A
Poetry Archive

Volume 1
By Alphabet and Beach
1998 - 2003

Frank Prem

Wild Arancini Press
2024

Publication Details

Title: A Poetry Archive -
          Archive Volume 1: By Alphabet and Beach - 1998 - 2003
ISBN: 978-1-923166-11-0 (p-bk))
ISBN: 978-1-923166-12-7 (e-bk))

Published by Wild Arancini Press
Copyright © 2024 Frank Prem
All rights reserved:

No part of this publication may be reproduced, stored in a retrieval system, or transmitted in any form or by any means, electronic, mechanical, photocopying, recording or otherwise, without prior written permission from the publisher and author.
A catalogue record for this book is available from the National Library of Australia.

Book cover design and formatting by WildAranciniPress.com

In order to become, first begin.

CONTENTS

A Poetry Archive Volume 1

Introduction 1
A - B 3
C - G 49
H - L 81
M - Q 103
S - Z 135
The Golub Suite 177
The New West 187
A Random Alphabetical 201
Whimsy 269
Beach and Water 287
After Words 319
    Index of Poems 321
    Author Information 329
    Other Published Works 331
    What Readers Say 333

A Poetry Archive Volume 1

x

Introduction

The A *Poetry Archive* series captures the great majority of formative poetic work undertaken by Frank Prem. Predominantly, the poems ci=ontained in Volumes 1 and 2 were written between 1998 and 2003, with instances of both prior and later work included.

The work in these volumes is raw and to some extent follows the development of Prem from an uncertain poet and through to a gradually more certain grasp of the craft.

The period from 1998 (and earlier) to 2003 covers a time of intense and extensive development by the poet with regular public reading at 'Spoken Word' venues, such as The Dan O'Connell Hotel in Carlton, as well as competition work and first publications of Prem's poetry in Journals, Newspapers or other Magazines.

The overall Archive - particularly Volumes 1 and 2 - is constructed to reflect themes where possible (such as Beach and Water, for example), with some work grouped in simple alphabetical listing.

Originally it was intended to publish each of Volumes 1 and Volume 2 as two books, hence multiple sets of alphabetially arranged poems.

Dates are given, where a record still existed.

A - B

a cloud beneath the cross

it was only a cloud
a small white fluff
on a flight-path below star points
hardly seen
against the glare of city lights

it shaped and re-formed
as it drifted
somehow purposeful
across the sky
paused for a moment
gathered itself
took in the whole
of the southern cross
then moved on

2003

a full confession

they came in large numbers
explorers
and foragers
searchers for shelter
and sustenance

dead
all dead
sprawled and contorted
and dead

two days later
a lone investigator
is searching

picking over the debris
prodding at the bodies
forensically sifting the air
for a cause
and a perpetrator

i am ready to confess
i will reveal all
conceal nothing

i killed them
each and every one
in cold blood

i have no time for ants
and their unsolicited reminders
of unwashed dishes
and benches that I have not wiped clean
for far too long

June 2000

a funny thing, memory

they said he had a photographic memory
the lucky bastard
he could tell you every little thing
whether he'd passed it on the street
looked at it in a picture
read it in a book
or whatever
every little detail
right out of the front of his head

except he couldn't feel anything
it was like he was cold
and empty of all the emotions
just had all these facts and images
he could reproduce if you asked him

must be terrible
to never be able to forget anything
might lead you to wandering
what alzheimer's is like
no I didn't mean that
I know that's a shit of a thing to say
or think

sorry

my memory is stuffed
sort of

I mean I get on ok and all that
but things just kind of pass me by
if I don't write them down

and that's a funny thing too
see

I write the stuff and then forget it
even real emotional things
and the *what* that *I* have to worry about
is to be careful what I read

Frank Prem

I've learned
you don't want to read too much
or it'll just bring you undone
and there's not much value in that

must be a funny business
being able to remember everything
and feel nothing

November 2002

a 'give-up' for love

she said

> love
>
> how're you going to know
> that you've had it
>
> if you don't give something up
>
> give something away
>
> you've got to lose something
> if it's going to be love
>
> I said

love

> well I gave up
> a piece of my self
>
> a piece I'd only just found
>
> I gave it away
>
> I was glad
> I was happy
>
> I guess it must have been love
>
> I didn't feel a loss
> I felt I was gaining
> and growing
>
> making myself something more
> until the end
>
> right until it was over
> then I was small again

she said

love
shhhh

you have to give
to touch greatness

a kind of love poem

Published in The Brown Critique (India) July - October 2001

i've been pretending
that i don't need
anyone to caress me
in the quiet of an hour
as time is passing
and moving outside the places
clasped in my reach

i know how foolish it is
to make out that castles
might keep against time
when they're eroding
fading away with each tick
of the clock

but i can't help it

if you reach
to hold me
i blink in your light
and then i need
to turn you away

when i'm alone
i feel so small

the world that's around me
is crowding me out

i feel surrounded
by people and things
that are out of control

hands that tremble
are a constant reminder
that i'm a fragile affair
balanced on the edge
of a blade

and even needing someone
can't change the outlook
of a solitary mind
that's confusing itself
from inside

perhaps it's better
if you turn your head

don't stay to watch
contortions of a fool disarrayed
by the burden
of trying to belong

2000

a lot 'o week

Tuesday and Wednesday are the empty days
no prospects to look forward to

Thursdays need at least a moment
to check numbers
and ensure the ticket is still good

Friday is a surge of hope held in the belly
a mind filled with bright lights and speculations

Saturday should be the big day
but I don't watch in the evening
my details are on a plastic card
and my evening is hopeful dreams

Sunday the papers are a temptation I resist
that is no way to discover something momentous

Monday every entry has been computer-checked
and any call on the telephone
could be the one that tells me

Tuesday is an empty day

August 2002

a nightshirt (for when it gets cold)

she laughed at me
said I was wearing a dress . . .

I'm not wearing a dress
a man would call this
a night shirt

I'd rather sleep nude
but some nights are cool
and when I feel a chill
I like to put the nightshirt on

but she laughed again
said that

>   *for sure it's a dress*

and that it looks very funny
especially around my stomach
especially around my . . .

I haven't seen her laugh so much
in a while
but I said

>   *it's a nightshirt*
>   *I only wear it*
>   *when I feel the cold*

a poet at war

He's like the bird
in a cage
in a pit
in a tunnel,
and he sings just to celebrate air.

Don't you love
to hear his tune,
the song of life?
Doesn't it make your heartbeat
sound a little stronger?

He is the bird in a cage
in a pit
in a tunnel,
where light won't fall
any more.

Where the air
has turned bad.

Can you touch the emptiness,
feel the silence grow?

He was the voice
at the centre of the heart.

He used to sing
to celebrate air,
loved the sound of a song.

Until the light fell away.

Until the air could not be breathed
any more,
and sound wouldn't come.

March 2003

a reading

yes, I will read for you child
but
there is a condition

when my voice slows and lowers
you must close your eyes

when you hear me

as   pulsing points

of   rhythmic

resonant

sounds

punctuated   by   pauses

you   must

s   l   e   e   p

May 2001

a shoe of frustration

I said

> *you 've misinterpreted me*
> *that isn't what I meant*

she said

> *so what did you mean then*

I said

> *I don't really know*
> *but it isn't what you thought*

she said

> *well that's a cop-out*
> *I think I've called you on this one*
> *and you won't admit it*

I said

> *no*
>
> *yep*

she said

> *I got you*

and then she walked

I thought

she's wrong
she's wrong
it isn't true

I may have spoken aloud
before I strode away
kicking a small shell-burst
of dust
up into the innocent air
with all the vented force
of an irritability I could hardly contain

viciously pleased that
at least
my tight-laced shoe
of only moderate destruction
had greater potency
at this moment of crisis
than would a moccasin

March 2003

a shooting star in emergency

I thought I saw a shooting star
not far above the height of my head
on the road outside the fence-line

it moved fast enough to create the illusion
but soon
too soon
became just a car
travelling the highway
lights reflected
on the overhead wires
of the electricified train line
and in a moment
it was gone

I feel I am a bookend to their relationship

I was there at the beginning
a dinner in a formal restaurant
jean-jacques
maybe the eatery-by-the-sea
maybe the other place
I no longer recall
but I was there
the day she and he came out together
that first time
the time it all began
to have a form and a shape

they married
both with the baggage
that comes with certain years
but they made their arrangements
and lived on through a decade or so

then our occasional convergence
constant friendship
rekindled as required
never a drama
always there if needed

I find I've gone on that way with so many
through the years
these '*certain years*'
that we who are now of that age
that was once the preserve of our parents
and their middle-aged friends
pass through on our individual journeys
to wherever it is we are travelling
the place where . . .

I don't really know

and now I am here
at the end
after their catastrophe
the death in the middle of
everything
that has been eked now
for forty-eight hours
while decisions about his lingering life
the viability of his organs

about the certainty of decease
and its aftermath
are made with solicitous care
about someone I once knew

and
while I am only a peripheral
yet I have my role
in the whole of this
process
the series of steps and consequences
for I cannot resist the call
to be the moral support
observer and dispassionate advisor

the ears and a heart

I was there when it all began
and I am here now
at the ending

A - B

it is not death that traumatises here
but that the simple man he was
would have wanted so much less
than he has been given

it is the excess that is cause for trouble
the tests and procedures
to confirm the knowledge
of a certain death inside his brain
and the absence of the soul
that must reside there

so much time before the pronouncement

in these things lies the pain
and the distress to all
the delay to commencement of grieving
and a closure

but it is nearly done
the beginning and the end
accounted for
it is late now and I have been affected
in the morning it will be completed
tubes removed
organs taken and despatched
to god knows where

some other victim in need
of a saving
the corpse prepared for viewing
with the best decency good-will can muster
for this man who died
two days ago
but has not yet
been allowed to stop breathing

I was there at their beginning
and now I will remain
until the end
the deposit of ashes
onto the moving water
of the bay

you know I thought tonight
for a brief moment
that I had seen a pair of shooting stars
skimming low
across the horizon of Station Street

I know it was only an illusion

only the reflection of a passing light
but for that fleet moment
I thought
it might be real

December 2002

a sound like moth wings beating

it is a long metropolitan road

a major artery

the car is rolling along
a hint of engine filtering through the cocoon

humming

he can hear it start . . .

a rapid-fire fluttering
like moth wings beating fast
and then it stops

the mirror up above his head
shows the back seat
between the passenger front head-rest
and his interior-pointing ear

there are blind spots
on the floor
and immediately behind him

traffic is moving

there it goes again
beating a little louder

someone is tooting
pointing
moving on ahead too fast

he tries to look around

the sound has stopped

he reaches with his hand
but there is nothing

then it starts again

he is traveling in the centre lane
but thinks he might like to pull over now

silence
the mirror says
the back is all in silence

he was starting to get nervous
but everything is quiet
he gives a little laugh
for being fooli

July 2002

a story for my lawyer

I wrote a story for my lawyer one day
when I was on the forty second floor
sitting in his office
waiting
to pay three-fifty dollars an hour
in six minute increments
for his time and his opinions

it was a beautiful tale
about the winding of the river

I could see the silver gleam
among the trees
and hills all the way back up to Mt Dandenong
and I wrote it down as it flowed
across my page

before he came into the room
to talk divorce
I had it written

I'd like to send the story to my lawyer
in a way it belongs to him
and his view from the forty second floor
but I doubt he'll ever see it
I can't afford the time he'd take to read it
at three-fifty dollars an hour
in six minute increments

January 2002

acknowledging original sources

the tattered green journal
(Collins Minute Book - Lexton Series)
speaks only the truth
in forgotten and painful ways
about the boy and about the man
he was trying to be

it details the places
where endeavour was not enough
the troubles that stole sleep
and the depths he could only fathom
by too freely imposing a mess
of confusion and despair
through the sad and angry lessons
that he taught to others
while still learning

it's all written down in scratchy pen
the words don't dare to lie
in an act of confession
by the author to the reader
as a whisper to himself
read down the years
at a time that suits reflection
on all the things he's done
and the place he's come to now
too late for restitution
but at least that character he wrote
I now acknowledge

July 2000

ad libbing

We're talking around in circles
We're talking about this (and that)
We're talking about moments
We talk in little twists

We're speaking of our day to day
We're speaking of our times
We're speaking without much to say
But this speaking is so fine.

We're saying what great friends we are
We're saying that we care
And we're talking about the fun we'd have
If only we were there

We're telling all our stories
And we're ad libbing, just a bit
We're sending little *'love you's'*
We are speaking - fuses lit.

August 1998

afraid of weather

You're embracing storms
but I'm afraid
of weather.
The rain and sleet of
knowing you
drive me down.
The thunder-rolls
grow louder with
each blackened
passing shower
and I stand in damp
surroundings
without a shelter
from the beating
of the wind.

January 2000

after 'till the next time'

but later
after the energy has gone
drained in a celebratory extravagance
super-high super-charged
and burned magnesium ignited
and you were so you
were so so good
and it rushed around your body
till you buzzed
and hummed fast really fast
but after
so empty that you rattle
like a rock in a can
you echo every time you have a thought
and the silence is screaming
nothing
you
only *you*
there's no one else
there's never anyone else
only you and it breaks
it kills
it's more than anyone
ought to have to take
and it's like that all the way
to the next time
the next time
bring on the fucking next time
bring it on

2002

alive

oh my *GOD*
there are times when I rattle
around this house
feels like a workout
walking one end to the other
but sometimes
when I swing around
the middle of the lounge
I raise my hands
I spread them wide
I don't touch a thing
or anybody
and I sing
like a devil in my lungs
wants to turn the air red
with a bellow of a song
YES
it's good to be free
in a space
I never have to share
yes
this air is mine to breathe
I love it when I feel
so alive

asthmatic refrain

I go through life quite sanely
As sanely as I can
Without too much excitement
For, I'm not that kind of man.
But, when it comes to bed-time
A funny thing occurs -
In my chest, a choking feeling
That grows from bad to worse.

My breath comes out all wheezy
And she asks, am I OK?
I reply, I need a puff,
Of that great inhaler stuff,
To help me on the way.
Oh, just a puff, a squirt, a gasp of it
Will help me keep my cool
So pass me over the Ventolin
(I'll follow all the rules).

Being breathless is a crazy thing
Completely occupies my mind
Upsets all my systems
And my way of life I find.
Now, there's just one thing to do
To stop me feeling queer
And, to show you're truly kind to me . . .
Please pass me the Ventolin, dear.

Well, I cope with that all right
It's just a part of life.
Like missing out on breakfast
Or getting nagged at by my . . . er . . . kids.
UNTIL - my nose begins to clog up
And my eyes both start to roll
Because with chest and nose all stuffed up
I can get no breath at all.
About then I start to panic
My mind it whirls away

And I know I need a puff
Of some great inhaler stuff
To see me through the day.
You know a puff, a squirt, a snort of it
Is really just the stuff
So lead me to the Beconase
(It's just like taking snuff!!)

Oh, it's the strangest of sensations
When your airways misbehave
The thing you must remember
Is to re-main very brave.
And please, don't go over-dosing
For that would be, Oh, so naive
Now squirt me over that Beconase.

Ah, me, when none of this will work
And life's a weary worry
There's nothing I can do
But breathe slowly - sad and sorry.
I've just contemplated suicide!
It's like breathing through a bone
When my doctor's worked a miracle
By prescribing Cortisone!!

July 1998

ATT #2 - almost sufficient

> Around The Table (ATT) was a call and response poetry circle with half a dozen poets from around the world each responding by writing a new poem after receiving the previous, in order around the table.

what was I thinking
I do not know

thoughts are like
the fish of the ocean
swirling and hazy

I float
mid-height mid-depth
I do not know myself
do not recollect
cannot project

I am
I must be
and that
is almost sufficient
almost

from my mid-being
I reach out

ATT #14 those hours

it's the chill hours
those darkness ones
when the bed hasn't been enough
and footsteps have led
to the place on the porch
where the stars are an expression
as brittle as feeling

those hours
when a curl of smoke unravels
while the goose-bumps rise
into encroachment by a shiver
from the surrounding silence

no-one should ask questions
in those hours
no good can come of it
and the answers won't stay till it's light

don't ask
go back to bed
sleep if you can
this is not the hour for that
just don't ask

ATT #20 - a heel on lino

I am thinking of her again
~

put the cardboard in the rubbish
scrape the plates
wash the dishes

the water's hot
suds are bright
almost the way they look
in ads on the tv

the lino on the floor
is cool against my heel
my sock has grown a hole
and I can feel leaves crush
as I wander in the darkness
to the outside bin

~

I can see light shining
as I look through the window
into my home
it's a sad little sight
empty chairs
television blaring out
to no-one there

I
am all there is
and the emptiness
signs to me
a whisper that I am not enough
not whole

ATT #26 the plot lost too

and the shape of the plot
is the measure of emptiness

I feel
you so far away
so alone

my hands occupy pockets
in the reflexive attitude
the slouch of depression
that comes with the donning of my first mood
in the morning

the shape of the plot
dissolves from my mind
with a stray deviation
into sunshine
then that too
is gone

until time passes

I will wait for the time to pass
wisdom it seems
grows slowly

~

if I stretched my hand
I could touch him
but I would not know
what to do
with the feeling
the sensation

I touched him before
once

I did more
held him close
and whispered into his ear

a dream

he grew afraid
was it of me
was it of himself
was it anything at all
or only a moment
that fell . . . into deep water

~

if I stretched out my hand
I could touch you

I almost feel
yoursensationyourhungeryourneedbut
I know my place
beside you

not close

not really so far

only the other side
of the planet

that's my position
I keep my arms
at my side
stay inside the barriers
I watch you through wires

I am just one
among the massing
of your numbers
until time passes

until *enough* time
passes

2003

ATT #33 - between this and the next

step here beside me
there is room that I have kept
between one moment
and next
it is cosy
and warm
step beside me
we can walk along
with the dog
take in the miles between then
and now
we might encounter ourselves
in the ways we were then
can you imagine the scene
I don't know
if I'd know myself
or would I know you
it was only a moment ago
just a bare time
yet
we've changed
oh lord we are in no way the same
as those people we were
and who will we be . . .
step beside me
we'll find out together
the things that a blink of the eye
holds in store
I'll hold you safe
if you'll hold me certain
between this moment
now

ATT #51 - growth by infusion

and it is like love
infused each time I
you
we
breathe
every small thing
is clean and new
every moment we are together
creating from nothing
from ourselves
every thought
when we are parted
directed to be shared
every touch when we lie together
it is all love
pervading everything
and we make it all the time
together
I cannot stop
would not want to
all the life that I know
has become a love making
and each time
I grow

baghdad rain, or a movie?

Would you like a cup
of tea, dear?
They're fighting in Iraq.
Sugars two,
milk for you,
no biscuits please
they make me wheeze
and did you notice
they're lighting up Baghdad?

Let's spend the evening
with the TV,
(are flares *all* green,
or is it just the sheen
from lenses made for night?)
because they've thrown a war
inside Iraq,
and they might be raining down
on Baghdad,
but we're all right,
safe here at home
the house is warm and I'm cosy,
are you, too?

If it gets too bad or noisy,
there's a truly excellent
movie
on channel
twenty-two.

March 2003

bath-time for boys

Two young men had a bath today.
Two young men splashed and played.
They went in dirty, and came out clean,
but the bar of soap was never seen.

They wet the floor and drowned their toys,
and accompanied the show with a lot of noise.
Their bodies were glowing, brightly pink
and they filled the bathroom up to the sink.

Their mothers said there would be a smack
if they didn't put the water back.
Instead of starting to scream and howl,
they mopped the floor with a dirty towel.

October 2000

beautiful pictures (1)

I don't carry photographs
I'm glad that I don't
pictures make me emotional
and I don't want to see you again
not the way you were
not with you smiling
in that dress you picked up somewhere
for a song

I don't want to see you
and I hate
I hate
I really *hate*
the way there's always one
of you
that hides somewhere
in the back of the sofa
glove box of the car
in the wallet in my pocket
that I get out every day
there's *always* one

you can't know
how I hate
pictures of you

beautiful pictures (2)

at the end of the day
after darkness
when the children are in bed
and the cleaning is done
her feet are in stockings
the couch in the lounge room
right next to the bookcase
with its identifications of birds
and species of native trees

collections of stories
that meant something once
long ago
not yet for the rubbish
too precious for garage sales
though their time may come soon
albums on the bottom shelf
on the covers a street scene
dogs in a rural setting
plain pale blue sky

selects one at random
looks at the index
in those days
she entered the details
of *where* and of *when*
before the photos
stopped being taken at all

can't remember clearly when that was . . .

why

a leaf through the pages . . .
some make her smile
some . . .
well
they hardly hurt any more
not much
barely at all

doesn't realise she is crying

until a sniff
and the sensation of a tear
rolling down her cheek

hugs it to herself
puts the album back on the shelf
where it came from
sniffles again
before going to the bathroom
to prepare for bed

believe the stars

There's a feeling in the placement of the stars tonight
They feel as if they're somehow on the move
They look as though they're at the point of taking flight
They look as though they must have got some news.

There's something in the placement of the Southern Cross.
There's something says it's showing me the way
There's a reason for the flicker of it's light, because
There's a reason in the shape that's on display.

The sky is sending messages of hope and light
The sky is sending messages of fate
The heaven up above is all alive tonight
The heaven up above is all awake.

Can you feel a new horizon start to open out?
Can you feel a new horizon stretching far?
Do you think there is a chance, and there can be no doubt?
Do you think the Southern skies know where we are?

Is it possible to trust the weight of stars at night?
Should we start believing night instead of day?
I believe the stars are telling us the time is right
I believe the stars are telling us OK.

I want to see the message from those Southern stars
I want to see their message in your eyes
I want to know they're shining deep inside your heart
I want to know that hope is free to rise.

I want to leap inside the brightness of the sun
I want to take you with me to the glow
Will you take a chance beside me if I choose to run?
That's the question in the stars I need to know.

October 1998

blood and feathers

it was a part of the wing
I suppose I knew it would be
for there could not have been
a different outcome
but still
hard evidence brought home
the futility
and bent me further
by a degree
or perhaps
it may have been two

when I was young

there were so many of us really
at that time in our lives
where there was something of experience
behind us
and unfettered potential ahead
the delirious age
that overflows possibilities
but is absent
a shred of mercy

would that we had been wary
but that was still a time away
and there was much for us

so very much

I knew it would be the wing
it is always the bloody wing

I knew that and I knew
that I should have let go
back there
on the cusp
before the bastard
ushered me on
to this

A - B

and the air thickened
and filled
with stray
red-spattered
feathers

April 2003

by silence

he was speaking
but I couldn't hear him
either too faint
or nothing
beyond lips and jaw moving
perhaps a conversation
inside his head
as loud as you like
but for me
nothing
and I find myself troubled
by silence

C - G

change of seasons

he dresses himself in the first long coat
of the cool season
the weather has fallen
the chill
is a drifting hover
above the ground

gloves
a scarf
the knitted woollen cap

the deciduous footpaths
a litter of brown leaves
the sky
fading skeletal finger-shadows
of bare branches
and disappearing cloud

the first mist materialises
with each exhaled breath
as he walks
hands in pockets
along the streetscape of new night
he is as empty
as the feeling of the season

~

a bicycle inquisition flashes past
all yellow reflections and strobe-light
examination of presence and purpose

the dog of indifference
sprays piss
then paws the ground -
oblivious -
at the corner of Corio and Maude
the light peering down
is a loneliness he avoids
by adherence to shadows

why does the man-shape -
behind a telling glow of cigarette ember -
dally against the fence
what purpose to its watching

move on

~

on the avenue of exposure
there are no trees
no cover
here it is rapid steps
and multiple following shapes
each drawn directly
from the placement of his feet
spreading out a pointer
to each available direction

there is no help here

he expected none

expected nothing

~

his shoulders have slumped

the further he has walked
the closer he feels
to the ground

there is no comfort in these places

above him
the darkness is complete
save for the twinkling lies
of faded representatives

they do not assist

~

in the light of a shopfront
he draws his cap lower
stops to look at the gaudy collection
vacuum cleaners
refrigeration
a compact disc rack

one silent wide-television
flashing images and colour

there is confusion here
move on

a vacant block
is home to a blackened gutted shell
that once sold yellow faux-leather divans
reclining lounge wear

an eyesore still

~

his nostrils are uncomfortable
sensitised
by the intake of cold air
to massage them
would require extraction
of hand from glove

he sniffs instead
turns the corner

there is no point in stopping

choosing between guitars

i almost wrote a poem about guitars
but i stopped myself in time
because i don't play

what i really wanted
to talk a little bit about
was choosing between new and old

a six string
and a twelve that was a gift
to a man with only one pair of hands
and a limit to the time and skills he can apply
to joy extraction and making pleasure

the twelve string is an exotic beast
and it makes a gorgeous sound
if you know what to do

how to stroke it and how to coax
and bend the notes till
they break somebody's heart
from an overdose of listening
to melody and sweetness

it can make you sound better

the six string is an old companion
to play with friends who want to sing along
to the same old words of the same old songs
we all know well
at three A.M. in the morning
because they've practiced for so long
with broken and smoky voices

hard to choose what to keep
and what to send away
when you only have
a single pair pair of hands

C - G

and a limit to what one man can do
to coax a little joy
extract a small pleasure
and make
a hard choice

August 2000

clues

there will be a clue in violets
when the perfume rises
to force a turn to halfway
across your shoulder
searching for a source
elusive and subtle

another will gleam
inside sunlight
arrayed to warm you
with a faint suggestion
of inner glow
emerging to transpire
porous and enlightened

there will be a third in silence
when absence is a comfort
honing the quiet senses
to enhance possibilities for receipt
of messages released
and wordlessly directed

there will be clues for you
if you should seek them
to aid your understanding
and a clarity of mind
that reaches through dilemmas
doubts and wonder

January 2001

colostomy song

I've got a colostomy,
at no cost to me.
The government pays for me.

It's a colostomy,
my bum's lost to me.
It's sewn up tight, you see.

It's quite diverted,
I'm disconcerted,
that all of this came for free.

(It's given me) a farting belly
that's as good as telly,
or the stereo's company.

I live at home now,
all alone now.
It's an awkward thing to be.

And there's no answer
about my cancer.
It's one of life's little mysteries.

(Bom, bom!)

July 2000

coloured sand dancing

pouches filled by coloured sands

a picture

lines poured by hand on earth
smoothed by a calloused man

enchantment songs of healing

the shaman

slow dancer of ancient steps
spelling pathways into spirit

image erased with the brush of a hand

scattered

rainbow sands to waiting air
take all harm away from me

June 2001

concert

it's a big big note
explodes across the mutter
of audience

striking them

the so-recognisable guitar
envelopes and quiets

speaks five notes

the keyboard
almost a whisper
against that powerful opening sound

then
again
the guitar

those five notes

the audience is hushed

reverent

a spotlight focuses
on the guitar
not the man

five notes

keyboard

it begins

January 2003

Frank Prem

confusing realities (a sound of thunder)

Good morning.
I am in Baghdad. It is one o'clock in the morning here.
The weather is fine. Except for the bombing.
Radio interview with a resident of Baghdad
25 March, 2003

I thought I heard the sound of thunder
but the clouds are light
and high

there is sunshine

it was a low threatening rumble
though I see a father and his son
trimming lawn-edgings
on the street
and it seems they
heard nothing

it was a sound like an impending storm
of hail
yet golfers are unhurried
playing out the ninth
on the course that parallels
the Aspendale wetlands

I was sure I heard the sound of thunder
but it must have come
from the television
from the Persian Gulf
where each night now
is a tempest
of unceasing noise

where the earth seems to tremble
and the lightning flashes fire
on and off
like a faulty neon signboard
that blazes right across the sky

C - G

until dawn

I think I better step
outside the house

think it's time
I breathed clean air

I need a better grip
on these
confusing realities

March 2003

craving

at odd moments I will imagine myself outside
I see this scene as though I am a separate person
a watcher
standing alone out there   in the act of
inhaling
it is almost as though I have in fact taken a drag
as though I am holding the very cigarette in my hand
almost as though I am ready to weep
the inhaled breath perilously close to jerking sob

but I do not weep
it is only a momentary visual memory
a hallucinatory flickering   a trick of addiction

conversation continues around me without pause
there is no waft of smoke above the gathering
but a descending sensation of failure
wreathing around me   an island of

    trickled

    thin

    blue

a lonely cocoon to silently embrace an urgent need
that only I can see   and taste

January 2002

currency

I had a dollar in the morning
when I first woke
the sun was currency-in-kind
fading with the day
until by evening I held nothing
but sparkle from a scatter of pennies
littered across the milky sky
out of the reach of an upraised hand
and the emptiness of my pocket

May 2001

Frank Prem

doing a shirt (steam)

lay the collar smooth and flat
crease it in the centre

    steam

sleeves left and right
straighten out the wrinkles

    steam

hook each shoulder on the taper
of the ironing board

follow from the buttonholes
around the back and to the buttons

    steam

drape it on the hanger
change the channel
sip a cold cuppa

    no steam

wander to the kitchen
break a dirty job to put the kettle on

    steam

July 2002

drowning slapnoea

too close

my body is held still
too close

I cannot breathe
weights surround me
pressing in

it's been too long

>   *I need to move*
>   *I need to push away*
>   *I need to move*
>   *I cannot move*

there is no inhalation

I am become
afraid

>   *go away*
>   *get off*
>   *give me a little room*
>   *I need to breathe*
>   *down*
>   *I'm going under*
>   *get away*
>   *get off*
>
>   *give*
>
>   *me*
>
>   *some*
>
>   *air*

thank god
the dark
is only night time

my eyes
perceive the crack of light
filtered through the yellow curtains
from the streetlight
I am gulping in
thankfulness

to sleep again

to sleep

May 2002

eyes awake

eyes awake at sunrise

no music for the dawn
only breathing sounds

air moving currents
to flow
as eddied streams
around true lightbulb North

half open at light time
action not scripted
slow frames unreel
a movie target
scene begun
silent picture

direction unknown

May 2001

faeces rag

Shit, shit, shit, shit
Mop, mop, mop, mop
Shit, shit, shit, shit
Mop, mop, mop, mop

There's faeces in the corridor
There's faeces on the chairs
Faeces in the carpet
And faeces on the stairs

There's faeces on the light switch
Faeces in my hair
Faeces on the handrails
And faeces left to spare

There's faeces in the ashtray
There's faeces in the air
There's you and me to clean it up
And shit just doesn't care

July 2000

family law

a bird shat on me today
I was under a tree
outside the solicitors office

it made a mess
of my hair and my coat
the way I present myself
to the world

Family Law sucks

August 2001

filling the quota

I have filled my quota
for today
but fell behind last week

I had my reasons

it was Easter
and even poets have times
when they cannot grasp
their thoughts
and wrestle them to paper

one poem each day
for a month
does not sound so very much
but it isn't always easy

and in any case
this
counts as an extra

April 2003

first week in the month

it is early May
the first week

this is the time of month for reflection
on the weeks just gone

on family

I think about my son
a long time gone
long time since we spoke
he is a traveller now in England
or perhaps it might be Europe
he said he'd like to go to Europe

I wonder if he made it

each month
sometime duriing the first week
I track his movements there
as I open the letter
with details of his credit card bill

lord it costs a lot to live in England

first week every month

family

May 2002

flying

the tasman's not an ocean or a sea
it's an aeroplane wing and clouds
under the sky

on maps they show water
but the only droplets i've seen
were in a plastic cup that came
with the plastic food and cold metal cutlery
about 30 minutes high

have you noticed
that there's never any birds?

it seems strange that i'm up here
and i haven't seen as much as a sparrow
i never do
when i fly

September 2000

fragment

sometimes the day is a song
but all you hear are fragments
of chorus and harmonies
but not the lyrics

some days I wish
I owned headphones

April 2003

from afar

There's discussion behind the trench lines,
some body saying words.
I can barely hear the voices and
I can't tell what I've heard in those
soft murmurs from across the waves
far . . .
so far . . .
spoken far away.

In a message from the cutting edge,
nuance hidden in the text.
I'm trying to read between the lines, but
the meaning's far too dense for me
to serve a sentence penned
far . . .
so far . . .
written far away.

I'm listening hard . . .

I'm reading you . . .

You're so far away.

January 2000

getting a grip (on nothing)

I grasped at a line of light tonight
must have shone
through a window of the car
from a street lamp or the moon
after I stopped moving

I clutched at nothing
was surprised for a moment
until I realised
then felt silly for a second time

when I was driving
I had a small hallucination
for the duration perhaps
of an eye-blink

I was touching a breast -
the last that I remember -
and I could feel it
familiar against the rasp of my face

I drew lightly on the nipple
to circumnavigate it
with my tongue
the way I used to do
to make it proud

then
it became obvious
and I hadn't crashed
though I could have
I believe I really could have

that was the first time

there was nothing there today
and I felt foolish
I am dreading
going to bed

February 2003

getting close to venice

the closest I came to venice
was a piece of glass
it was blue
transparent
placed in the window
of the newspaper shop
a decanter and six cups
made to do something
god knew what
I bought it for my mother
and it still resides
on a shelf in the lounge room
dusty
untouched
a reminder of the wide world
seen
when I was still small

November 2002

goodnight

the days are taken up
almost absent-mindedly
with tasks of work and with idle hours
papers to read
lunch to be consumed
coffee

evenings are a greater challenge
little to do
but endure the bright flicker
and booming sound of the television

the moment of going to bed delayed
a little too long
almost as though it threatens
though this is not so
for the bed is a comfort
and the warmth of blanket and doona
are both an embrace and a relaxation

crime fiction postpones sleep
in a persistent pattern of long standing
for which there is no good reason
beyond occupation of time until weariness
and the light goes out

there are no fears in the darkness
no ghosts to confront
when the yellow bulb is extinguished
sleep will come easily enough
it is only with the movement
towards the bedside

and the switch on the far wall
to allow the day finally to end
that I hear myself say *'goodnight'* out loud
to an empty space
and feel a moment of bewilderment
before touching the switch

    good night

October 2002

got no rhythm

(a-do   do)
(a-doo-doo-doo-doo)

it's no good
(a-do-do-do)
i can't write rhythm
it's no good
no good at all

i can hear the sounds
and feel the beat
enough to make me tap my feet
dance around in
this mind of mine
music playing all the time

but it's no good
if i can't write rhythm
(a-do-do-do)
no rhythm
(do-do)
no rhythm at all
(d'oh!)

December 2000

H - L

habits die hard

i think of her sometimes
when i'm reading over letters
or recalling places i have been
things i said
once upon an age ago

and then i wonder
how is she now
does she still look just the way
that i remember

there's an image in my mind
that takes the place of photographs
we took no pictures
parted with only words
and a few small deeds
as the basis for memories
but sometimes my habits won't die
and i think of her

June 2000

hammered gold and gilded tin

It is a grail of sorts, the quest
for possession of a small
but precious and growing thing,

the evolution of a child.

The taste of truth is crafted
in a cup of beaten gold,
shaped plain and unadorned
of false or burnished pride.

The cup of venality
lies coated in thin enamel.
Gilded stuff, poor of substance.
Pretty, gleaming, shallow.

Which will nourish
the thirsty young?

From which a sip
for the future?

Hammered gold or yellow gilt?
Elixir or sugared syrup?

March 2001

I know

When I was just a little boy, I knew.
When I was just a very little boy I knew.
Oh when I was nothing more than a baby child,
crawling with my hands, running wild,
when I was nothing but a baby child, I knew.

When I was just a gangling youth, I knew.
When I was just an awkward, youth, I knew.
Oh, when I was nothing but a stripling lad,
gazing at the moon, going to the bad,
when I was nothing but a stripling lad, I knew.

When I grew up, an upstanding man, I knew.
When I grew up as a fine-standing man, I knew.
Oh, when I wore the badge of a suit, tie, and hat,
taking on the world, with this and with that,
when I wore the badge of a suit, tie, and hat, I knew.

Right through my life, from the early days,
I've known.
Right through my life from the very early days, I've
known.
Oh, right from the time I took my first breath,
breathing so hard, till there wasn't any left,
right from the time I first took my breath, I've known.

Tomorrow could be anything to me, I know.
Tomorrow could be almost anything to me, I know.
Oh, who can tell if the day after this,
might lead to disaster, or shine sweet bliss?
No-one can tell about the day after this, but I know.

I know.

1999

if a rialto crumble

if I were at the bottom
of a heap of Rialto crumble
after terror from the Victorian blue skies
had struck a blow against our way of life
and understanding
perhaps an Ansett jet
creating havoc and tasting revenge
to highlight the injustice done
to thousands
thrown onto the wreckage
of an aviation scrapyard

if I were at the bottom of that pile
of junk and twisted debris
would there be a camera crew from CNN
taping in the night
and would America stop
in the middle of it's doings
stay glued to watch my drama on the TV
the way that I feel compelled
to watch them
in their struggle
and through their grieving

September 2001

if the sky should fall

this is really a song but
I don't think anyone from my time
can get their tongue and lips
around the words and tune
it's about things we've never seen
it's about

Pero the one struck from out of the blue
of a clear and bursting sky
that fell down on naked heads
guess he was in the way
guess he never saw it coming I
don't believe that we you and I
or anyone of all of us
saw it coming down
maybe we never do
Pero was the one too slow
to dance away from harm
a little too close

I read to you when we were courting
songs and psalms and calls to come
into my open arms
so you could hold me tight
and we could combine flames
light the sky on suburban nights
empty drained of all promises
except for the two of us
and the words we whispered
to the moving restlessness
of a Chelsea beach

where was Pero then
when salted waters lapped our feet
when we played at house
and when we made a home
I guess he was on his way
guess he didn't know

I don't suppose it really would have
changed a single thing
if the sky decides to fall
it will take out who it wants to

this was meant to be a song
but I don't feel like singing I
can't touch music in the air
and I don't quite believe in it anymore
because I have clapped my hands
but there's no Pero crawling
himself up to stand in the dust
and tell me: it's only a bad dream
raise your voice up to the sky
and sing for me

remember when I needed you
the time that I was falling a little down
and a long way apart . . . do you recall
it was the day I thought disaster
had called me from the past
it turned out only a scare but you know
it felt as though it really happened then
I guess I must have known that one day
it would happen even then

I don't think Pero is coming home again
think he's gone this time for good
beneath the fire and smoke and dirt
underneath the rubble piles
they used to bury people under mounds
they used to burn their bodies
and I think that Pero is a funeral mound
I think he is a pyre

I don't want to sing right now
I want to go to sleep

September 2001

illumination - my turn

i remember playing children's games
pistols in the yard at home
we would fight to see who'd be black
and who was white

you could always aim much truer then
i could never shoot so straight
i would die and you would win
then we'd get the call to go in for dinner

sometimes i hated your certainties
always on the side of right
never wrong and never room
for any doubt to cloud you

looking in your eyes i see you now
tired from the weight of light
your shoulders sag low
and you stumble under burden

listen   i will play a song for you
while i envied   you made me proud
to stand beside you   to fight and die
no child desired for more

you and i can play our games again
this time from a bench and chair
fire away your righteous best shot
i will illuminate your errors

it is my turn

September 2001

in absentia

sometimes I can feel myself dying
not by the year with the creeping of age
but by the minute   every second
I look around and something is gone   something is changed
and I wonder where I was when it happened
I am away so often
I think I might be dying in absentia

January 2002

interior designs

the place I live is boxes now
scattered in a disarray through every room
some I have not looked at or opened
in all the weeks I have been here

but I will move on soon
to a place of my own
my first place of my own
with none to share it
no-one to take over rooms
or to crowd me into corners

and what will I do
to place my mark there
I have asked myself
what sense of character will I impart
how will I define my tenure
in this
my first solo abode

I do not envision paintings on my walls
I have no great artistic acumen
and must leave that to others

I am no accumulator of knick-knacks
have never known what to place
upon a mantelpiece
apart from a single statuette
a poetic muse in bronze

all my sentimentality
is slid between the edges
of plastic envelopes
in albums of poetry
the way others take photographs
one album for each year that passes
my diversions are contained in books

I believe I will line my walls with bookshelves
and I will scour the second-hand stores
for every novel I have read
that has ever suggested itself to me
for a second reading

kaminsky and block
greenwood and corris
the crime stories that rise
one clue above the rest

gormenghast and mr pye
bilbo and gandalf
the atreides and the harkonnens
the fantasy and future worlds
that have always seemed so much more tangible
than this place

h e bates small stories of the heart
melancholy beauty to haunt the soul
and to show a man how to write

don camillo and peppone
battling in the small world of the po river

I will haunt the second-hand bookshops
in a search for treasures read before
and find a place upon my bookshelves
to show the words that have shaped and diverted me
the places of escape

and in the night when I sit alone
after a meal or before sleep
I will read — not from my shelves
stacked with the words that have claimed me

but from the public library
searching for another tale
to make me think one day
I should find a home for this
on my bookshelf

October 2002

it's valentine's

it's valentines
I'm watching stars
at twinkle right above my head
they seem happy there
as far as I can tell

the bodies on the street
are coupled up
and walking close

contentment
in the state of mind
that slow strolling
of their feet reveals

they're taking time
on valentines

the people I was with tonight
said we must be
the last unromantic ones
who leave partners behind
to amuse themselves alone
while we
do the annual let's
get together once a year
this time
on valentines

now they've all gone home to bed
and I
could do that too

I guess I will

but first
I have some stars to watch
at twinkle
right above my head
they seem happy there
this valentines

February 2003

just friends

friends
I watch you
while we're eating at a restaurant

we talk a lot
about the folk we know
the things we did when
we were only kids
people that have died

friends
I can see the girl you were
the woman here
leap across the middle years
make it all add up
to the you I know
as comfortable
as friends can be
we can go anywhere
in our talk
good friends that we are
we roam across a universe
but skim
across those fleeting days
when we were more
don't talk about that so much
but
I stay glad
we found our way
to being friends

good friends

. . . sometimes I remember
the way you shivered
inside out
it made you laugh
you made me laugh
you said that only happened
because it was so good
we were very good

. . . sometimes I remember
wonder why
we're friends

letters and words

two *fuck you* letters in three weeks
ex- and lover . . . . . maybe ex- and ex-
ignore them both
one because it doesn't matter anymore
the other because there are things yet to say
words to be spoken
through a trembling chin
a shaking voice
and the moisture collected in the corner
of an eye

not *love you*   that would be much harder
these are the simpler words
of commitment
of want and need to share lives
words of asking

if the answer is *yes*
love you will follow
if not
I will read my *fuck you* letters in the evening
and ponder

February 2002

lighthorse man in my collection

I have a stamp in my collection
that shows a blue hole in the head
of a lighthorse man
with a feather in his cap
and the face of a young man
in a strange place
doing something he doesn't
really understand

it's a rarity
of sorts

not the man out of his place
they've been doing that
to young men
for a long time now

the blue hole in his head
was only one in every fifty
and I had to join a queue
to have my chance
but I wonder what his odds were
in that dusty place so far away
before he came to reside in my collection

March 2001

like a stereo out of hell

it's taken six months
but now the stereo works
and the speakers are sounding fine
they're resounding to the cry of a *bat*
out of hell
filling the house with life
and while the neighbours might have thought
I was a quiet sort of man
who never knew how to say *boo*
the stereo works and Meatloaf and me
are out to prove that's not true

I'd forgotten how much I need to fill up
my space
how the music can force me to dance
unresisting in its beat as I swan about
the place
arms in the air
a swagger in my step
hips that have learned how to sway

but he took the words right out of my mouth
swear on my heart that's the truth
I was just about to sing the song
but I got no further than a lick of my lips
and the thought of some girl's lingering kiss
when the chorus drowned me out

but now the stereo's back
there'll be time for all that
meanwhile I'm prancing all across the floor
like a man revved up
without a place he can go
by a stereo screaming in a banshee wail
the music of a bat out of hell

April 2003

liqour kiss

Hold that sweet bottle
Hold it close, to your lips
Smell the sweet liquor
Taste it . . . little sips.

Catch the hot feeling
Roll it on your tongue
Bathe in heat intentions
Taste it . . . liquor song.

Close your eager eyes
Take, a larger swallow
Drink it to the limit
Taste it . . . more to follow.

Mmm, love that sweet bottle
Holds taste good as this
Drink with abandon
Taste it . . . liquor kiss.

October 1998

long distance love affair

Long distance love affair

I love you on the phone.
I tell you that I care.
I wish that you were home.

Long distance love affair

I think of things to do.
It's empty for me here.
So lonely without you.

Long distance love affair

Do you dream me in your sleep?
Are your dreams something we share?
What images do you keep?

Long distance love affair

I wake up in the night
I call to you by name
You vanish with the light.

Long distance love affair

I'm crying all the time
You hurt me through and through
Is loving you a crime?

Long distance love affair

I wish you'd let me go
I need you more and more
That's the only thing I know

Long distance love affair

You travel overseas.
See the pretty's there.
Do they pleasure and appease?

Long distance love affair.

July 1998

M - Q

master of nothing new

here's the master of nothing new
coming down the road

how's it going
what's the goss around
nothing much
nothing changes

it's the same old rhythms
same-same days

got a note from charles today
asked me how i'm doing now
haven't thought of him in all these months
so long he's almost disappeared
i've got no time
for filling in blanks
on paper lines
just to say i'm still the same

i get up
in the morning
wear the clothes
still labelled *yesterday*
do the hair and teeth and all that stuff
before they melt away
from the mirror
on the decoration wall
that shows my pictures
as a reference
to progression
from a bright young thing
to a something else

well i don't know

i don't know
maybe the next look
can reveal the *who* i am

nothing new to report today
nothing new ever happens

catch you later
i'll see you around
keep an eye out
for changes

May 2000

middle winter blues

it may be because I've stopped
observing clouds
the bundled lump-mountains of cumulus
streaked cirrus and dotted spots of fleece
that populate the sky have not held
my attention
and though the bled-grey watercolours
I noticed this morning
were interesting at the time
they have gone now
and all there is left to see is a dirty
half-darkness
broken by occasional faded blue and filter sun
not worth the placement of pen on paper

Dominic is pleased to hear my news
for the second time since I told him
I've enjoyed a free latte
at the Chelsea Central
I don't know if he is like this
with all his customers
but he seems genuinely pleased
that I will be returning
to live in this area close enough
to be a *regular* again
I think he may have taken to me
because I claim to be a poet
because I gave him a framed poem
about himself
and about the café and the street
for the Christmas before last
he will be a neighbour when I move

I am weary of this winter with its low misery
I have hardly stepped casually from the house
in two months
not counting a week spent in the sun
on the Gold Coast
three degrees too cool to approach perfection
perhaps it is a winter depression
that has crept over me

sneaking up through the days and nights
of July
to settle white like drifted frost or dandruff
on my shoulders
sunshine seen beckoning through the window
is a deceptive lie
there is no warmth in it
and those wretched clouds
that I no longer notice seem to hover in wait
ever-ready to replace brightness with a pall
that arrives in the blinking of an eye
it could be because of that

August 2002

miss it a bit

it's not that I want
someone to share my bed
oh no
it's such a pleasure do you know
to be able to stretch out
in any which way
and meet no obstructions
such a pleasure

and it's not as if
I need someone telling me
every morning
that I was cutting trees all night
so loud
and couldn't be shifted
or shut up
no matter how many times
I was prodded in the ribs
or spoken to
I can do without that
for sure

and being hot
when she's cold
and cold when she's hot
it isn't as if
you couldn't live well
if that didn't happen

and you know
as it is now
I can just waltz around the house

if I wake in the night
make a little noise
whatever
never have to think
about anyone else

go back to bed
when I feel like it
lovely

but do you know what
it's watching a woman in my arms
when she's asleep
just looking at her
while she doesn't know
it's happening
you can see so much
sort of absorb the stuff of her
through your eyes

I do miss that

a bit

February 2003

mizzle down

the clouds have broken, mizzle down
soft on my hand, a tattoo fall
from the sky, to touch me cold
in an erratic beat
for as long as I can stand the chill
and the bite of a wind that doesn't care
if I am standing here
around me is an easy path

for the indifferent breeze
is wrapping droplets all about me
like a blanket of mizzle down
as the grey descends
to cover morning, I must go
away, inside a day of electric lights
heating and sad glances
through window panes

feeling mizzle down

April 2001

morning metaphor

don't forget that morning is a metaphor
for any time the darkness fades
and you catch a glimpse
of the faint light of dawn

don't forget that it harbours promises

the night can stretch to the limits
of your coping
but come the hour
come the minute
or the moment
the black will fade to grey
and then
the light comes
to show a place to start
tomorrow

2000

moving air

I have assumed the position suggested:

legs wide in a side-on stance
arms stretched out
forward and back
hands cupped to hold:

but
I cannot properly grasp
the weight of air for transfer
from where it is
to where it should be
it is only arms and my hands that move
flow is absent

I am feeling for the wind
to guide me

April 2001

nervousness

>*I can't really
>see that there's any reason for it*

~

we are at a wedding
the bride is late
the slow-step up the aisle
is a jig of twitches
tears
beaming smiles
a barely contained agitation

~

she half-whispered

>*I organised mine
>did all the planning
>made sure everything was attended to
>then let it happen
>good planning leads to good results
>and an absence of concern
>so you can enjoy your big day
>I certainly enjoyed mine*

~

the bride is dancing up and down
on the balls of her feet
in front of the priest
beside her almost-husband

~

thoughts have strayed to my own wedding
years ago
numb as frozen as a carved statue
while shaking like a leaf

barely able to respond
to rehearsed prompts and cues
bewildered and overwhelmed
mindless with fear

I thought of others
who never believed the day would come
never believed they'd find their match
those conscious of the watching gaze
of a judgmental family
a judgmental world

those waiting at the altar
wondering if something has gone wrong
those donning the veil
wondering if the decision
has been the right one
those with a secret held close

~

the solemnity of the occasion
has been disturbed
there is a titter passing
through those gathered here today
for the priest has had a small stumble
in performance of the ceremony
he has married the bride to christ
instead of in christ
it occurs to me that such an error
could have consequences
his eyebrows are doing backflips to compensate

~

nope

she muttered

*there's no excuse for being nervous
you just have to make it happen
and then you get on with it*

2002

not really fragile

it's only incidental breakage
i'm not really fragile
perhaps inclined to accident
and bruises
that show much more
than i could wish for

long sleeves and make up
in a coat of darkest blue
are camouflage
discretion
an air of knowledge
and self control

over what's *my* business
keep away i've not issued
open invitation
for casual observers
of a spectacle
event or lurid sideshow

don't you think you might be
a little fragile yourself?
i notice that you
sometimes hold your breath
when you look at me

maybe a bruise or two
gives a twinge
when you see me wearing blue
marks or faded yellow places
that hardly offer pain
with the passage
of my time

are you strong enough
to carry yourself
in long sleeves and make up?

or are yours
bruises that won't hide
when you're
a little bit fragile?

July 2000

observing beautification (through force of habit)

the sound of concrete cutting
is incessant
fluttering my eardrums to suggest
excessive decibels
I am probably doing harm to be so close
to these men and their wailing masonry blade

a momentary pause brings relief
the sound of passing traffic
is relatively hushed although
at other times it would seem intrusive
contrast brings perspective
and I would welcome more of such a change

these men in their red and yellow jackets
and earmuffs stand centred in the road
guiding the flow of traffic
while machinery moves around them
seriously intent on the beautification of this street
though you would not think that
just from watching
and suffering their screeching clamour

I am not here studying a changing streetscape
or the industrial habits of local council men
toiling through their workload this day
I am here only through the force of habit
another cigarette will see me through
and I will be on my way

the noise has stopped
it is time for me to go

October 2001

a day in the life - october 4 - NPD

October 4 2001 was National Poetry Day in the UK.
Poets were asked to write their day episodically. This was my day.

Cheltenham - Melbourne, Australia -
6:30 am

my eyes are open   it's half past
six o'clock
why am I awake on a day off work?
well there are accounts to do and the mail
to collect from Chelsea   back
before nine
to mind the overnight stay children awhile
but they'll be gone before lunch
and the house will settle down

~

Cheltenham - Melbourne, Australia -
lunchtime

paperwork goes on and on   no end
I'll stop for a bite and a moment with Sandy
four children now and another overnighter
this isn't what I'd hoped for from the day
Robin wants a ride to get here
he'll stay for a week and that's fine
I'll find the time
to collect him somehow and Tracey says
yes   she'll come to dinner please

~

Moorabbin - Melbourne, Australia -
5:00pm

hey Franky
can you get some onions and coriander
while you're on your way home for dinner?
everything's done you don't have to worry
the kids'll be fine and Robin's not a problem
don't you love our house brim full of people?
lamb curry and wine with the video on
in the back room for the short ones
it'll be just fine you know

~

Cheltenham - Melbourne, Australia -
11:30pm

the kids must have really been tired
they went out like a light   four voices
stilled
in a moment & Tracey has a man in the wings
it's about time something like that happened
what a wonderful night we had   so good
to have children and friends in our lives
it's almost time to dim the lights goodnight
goodnight

~

Postscript - Cheltenham - Melbourne,
Australia

we do not have a national poetry day here
at least not one that I can easily discover
it seems a sad thing   only a very small sadness
not ranking with the great events
of today's world

but there are few in this country
that will share
a wonderful day in the wonderful lives
of a handful of poets writing their humanity
in places all over the world
and that is a small sadness
for me at least

October 2001

on introduction

and would we learn more
with a professional approach
by perhaps applying the tenets of psychiatry
utilising the forms of intake assessment
for first meetings
the basis for a grounding
at the point of introduction?

exposure of the presenting situation
the *why* of now
followed by personal background information
childhood history and milestones
genogram and developmental issues
within the family
pre morbid personality and shaping tendencies
use of drugs and other illicit substances
the existence and extent of a support network

a quick run through the mental state
assessment
stream of thought and content
orientation to person place and time
appearance   behaviour
and the flow of speech
contemplation of the presenting mood
and affect
perceptive state   intelligence
and cognition
rapport with the interviewer and insight
a considered formulation and conclusion
with recommendations

perhaps I should be more professional
perhaps I should take trouble to learn more
perhaps it would be safer

March 2002

paper aeroplanes

these are paper aeroplanes
and I'm flying
half a loop-the-loop
and slide down to the ground
elegance
and grace upon a current of
the finest air

until a strutted wing turns me
from fly to dive
in an awkward way
with a nose turned to up-set
angle wrong
and a fast descent
in harder air

they are only paper aeroplanes
parked below a
fold-down futon storing
dust, a shoe
and crumpled paper
from a fun some time ago
and stagnant air

February 2001

perfume?

do you wear perfume
I find I can't tell
it must be delicate to the senses
and gently applied
because it never interferes
with the smell of you

sometimes when you're away
I can taste it in my air

May 2000

plastic spirits

I take my spirit from a plastic cup
yellow liquid in a white surround
and imagination to make it taste

not quite what the distiller hoped
but Scotland's far away from here
and I'll have it this way even though
the sound of teeth on the rim
grates hard on my nerves

shot through and watered down
a half an inch is all that's left
to hell with plastic crumple cups
straight out of the bottle now

bouncing round my feet to break
but I'm already half away
spirits warmed and temper stayed
deep into the shadows
black and gone

April 2001

plat-ing

he doesn't know what to say
sometimes catches himself
in the middle of a platitude
telling her she would be all right
it would all be well
she'd be back on her feet
and doing all the usual things
in no time at all
and it's worse when he notices she's agreeing
with a nod
when he knows full well
she doesn't mean it
doesn't think it's ok
she believes and he knows
life came to an end
and it'll never be the same
but he doesn't know what to say
sometimes it's easier to deal with each other
in platitudes

2002

politics personal

look there's just no point
in talking about it
you have your view
and I can see
nothing I say is going to change your mind
I have my view
and I know your arguments
will not sway me

you will go away
and act upon your views
involving me -
whether I agree or I do not
in their outcomes and implications -
I will seethe
frustrated
and glow red through shame

June 2002

pot pourri

I've heard that
if you gather
the coloured petals
of sweet blooms

the ones releasing
perfume that
can reach
inside your mind

that every coloured shape
will keep it's
beauty

and when you hold it close
it can transport you
to another place
and another time

to when the sun
was rising warm
and skies were blue enough
for simple pleasures

like appreciation
of a rose
and the wonders
of the garden

but it isn't true
and all I find
is new ways for
bruising blossoms
and with the clumsiness
of a coward
I'm crushing flowers

March 2000

predator

> *you are a predator*

the tone was vehement
voice trembling

> *you prey on people like me*
> *single mothers*
> *vulnerable*
> *you think it's ok*
> *just seduce and then fuck off*
> *at a hint of involvement*
> *a fucking predator*

he held her while she sobbed
into his shoulder
wondered

> *am I?*
> *is that what I do?*

thought about the ache of months
since he had held someone

why had he come here today?

she struck him a light blow
of fist into shoulder
moved away from him

> *why did you come here today*
> *you bastard?*

he looked past her
to the wall

    sorry

stepped through the door
heard her voice

    no

a sound of weeping

    (see also: The World's Greatest Lover and The Reviewer)

February 2003

pretensions

I met a man last night.
I'd known him, briefly
many long years ago.
In just a moment of conversation
I was back.
A shallow, unformed fool
of a young boy/man.

Life is a strange place
and my pretensions
don't really fool anyone.

October 1999

prickling eyes

first it is a prickling of the eyes
perhaps a sleep would help?
but no there is a need rising
held below the diaphragm
rigid in the short intake of breath
controlled to pass the tightening
stricture forcing out a lumpen shuddered gasp
that lets a droplet overflow
and a sound so deep and torn
that this must be a man
caught in a despair   that wonders why
and cannot stop   cannot stop
when a man begins   he may never stop
until the world has fallen down
until there is nothing left
exhausted by the empty weakness
of responding to a prickle of his eyes

2001

S - Z

search for my soul

mostly they are brown and dry
except for small holes
where the laces thread
to keep the tongues inside
and the leather hugging close
around my size 10 feet
but this time there's a fault in one
I can feel a damp sensation
at the bottom of my sock
I am adjacent to a puddle
but the water level's rising
and if it saturates my trouser leg
I could be at risk from rising damp
I do not trust the weather agents
who say today was fine
and tomorrow will be better
except for water on my knee
I think there's rust
forming on the key ring in my pocket
perhaps they've all corroded
and won't open up the door
so I can escape the creeping tide
that laps a first touch
the one I hate
around the goolies makes me shiver
up and down my spine
and almost ill with apprehension
that naval battle may be launched
in the vicinity of my belly
perhaps it's submarines
below the yellow shirt
and teddy bear tie I wore
to work today

I need a bottle to keep this note dry
and a cork
floating by below my chin
the gutter must be overflowing
I may need to send out
for a snorkel and a face mask
though perhaps as I am drowning
even my life
will flash before me
from the moment of conception
to this last over-beating
gulp of moments
I have heard it can be spiritual
that a man may find his soul then
and surely I could use mine right now
because these wretched shoes
are letting in the waters
of the world

October 2001

shoes

this morning i found your shoes
unexpectedly
they were tucked away
behind the end of the futon

I wonder
what you're wearing now

May 2000

short-term tenancy

the house is a barren prospect
an idiosyncratic testament
to the needs and vagaries of past occupiers
due for demolition and gentrific metamorphosis
in an area of nouveau potential

the rooms reek of an invasive disinfectant
the landlord has gone to some lengths
to disguise lingering smells
that ooze from cracked walls
and spreading floors
a vague presence of rot
the pervasive odour of sweat
as though a dozen generations of testosteroned tenantry
viewed concepts of hygiene
with disdain

bare boards
naked timber benches
cobwebs and cavities
burnt-out lightbulbs
boxes

his boxes are everywhere
a disarray of packaging
bed linen in the lounge
books and paraphernalia in the main bedroom
the one where the light switch
does not respond
they will not be unpacked
this is short term-only

he will move on soon

September 2002

single drek

will it be a book tonight
or the tele
dinner was a table
for one facing the window
at the noodle bar

no point calling up a friend
it's saturday
there's no-one home
and it doesn't do
to wear the welcome down

lie down on the settee
remote control to change the show
nothing worth a second look
nothing to talk about tomorrow
and no-one to say it to

leave the front door open
hear the traffic flow
up and down
this dead-end street
it's good to know
there's life out there
god knows
everything has died in here

could have gone out
to the singles bar

for anybody
over twenty-eight
but how do you join that exuberance
how ever do you change
into a body more attractive

it's looking like an early night
the telephone is silent
no-one thought to give a call
but hardly anybody
has the number and anyway
you look at it
this single life is only
drek on paper

November 2002

single male shopper

he looks clean enough but
seems crumpled
as though he could not escape the wash
but somehow foiled
the iron

perhaps lost
or just vague
distracted
as he propels the trolley
up and down
each and every aisle
as if he has no list
of what is needed
but hopes to know it
when he sees it

needles
sewing needles

should he
or shouldn't he
the decision requires
inordinate consideration
and study
perhaps he's peering not at price
but into the future
trying to picture himself
re-attaching a button
that is yet to unravel from a shirt-sleeve
imagining a domestic situation
with himself as protagonist

no
nothing for the laundry

more decisive in meat
where a schnitzel special
is particularly attractive
always easy in the fry-pan
two packs
one for the freezer

vegetables
warrant hardly a glance
another sign perhaps
of his status
grapes though
yes
no problem

soft-drink cheese-slices
salami-smallgoods
packet of gummy bears
milk and yogurt

pre-pack fettucine
a microwave sauce
one quiche and six meat pies
freeze him in the chill section
cause him to pause   to visualise again
this time
the inside of his own freezer
at home

toilet paper toothpaste
paracetamol shampoo
no condoms
no socks
no jock-ettes
no razors
no soap
ah
apple juice on special
at the corner of the aisle

S - Z

steers to the counter
the only counter
where cigarettes are sold
a carton of gaspers
to conclude

on credit please

March 2003

sleep in his head

sometimes he wonders
if this time will be a long one
sometimes he feels too much alone
there's a feeling flows over
from the depths and out of nowhere
washes places he thought long gone
shivers deep into his bones
as he stares up at the night
it always seems quiet at home
beneath stars that cold-flicker
without interest in a solo
wonders where meaning has gone

he can call to the night-sky
that hovers right above him
and speak about doubts that he knows

he can talk-back at the tv
with its blare and flash-strobing
tell it the script is unfair

he can spit back at the frypan
on the cooktop in the kitchen
that sometimes he'd like to explode

he might mention to the bed
as he sits before the lie-down
that he never liked sleeping alone

then silence all thoughts
in the soundless bitter darkness
for sleep whispers the past in his head

sleep whispers past
in his head

April 2003

unfamiliar affections

af·fec·tion (ə -'fek-shən) (P) Pronunciation Key (-fkshn)
n.
A tender feeling toward another; fondness. See Synonyms
at love. Feeling or emotion.
Often used in the plural: an unbalanced state of
affections. A disposition to feel, do, or say;
a propensity. Obsolete. Prejudice; partiality.

and I am wholly wholly given over
to these unfamiliar af·fec·tions
in my awareness of your presence
the absence of a key to you
unbalanced -fkshn

2002

snapping pictures

he doesn't like the snap of pictures
evidence someone might use
to change his life
graven imagery of good times had
remind him of a promise he made
not to let his guard slip
and a frown can be a riddle
hiding signs of innocence
and simple pleasures

some things are much easier
if they're hidden in the deep and
darkest places turned away from the glare
of a flashing light and a record
not meant for family albums
or reminiscences of fine days
and sunshine on a stretch of sand

time spent in the breakers
might be a source of harm to someone
in a courthouse far away
when the climate gets much colder

September 2000

staying

She asks me to stay
until the others have gone.
It's a ritual played out
even if we're yawning.

Sometimes we'll dance,
almost until early light,
as vague reason suggests
we should keep going on
and neither of us wants to stop yet,
or to take a slowing breath.
We want to squeeze out every moment
until there's nothing left, no remains,

for we've had those conversations
about potential sudden demise,
and agree on no ever-afters
that are only ever glib lies and we've watched
the come-and-go   of too many friends
who never stayed to say good-bye,
thrown the clods of rich, brown earth,
weeping like children at their gravesides,

and she said to me

> *'If ever . . .*
> *If you should ever . . .'*

She said

> *'Just don't,*
> *all right?'*

All right.

*'Wait here awhile, until I
tell the others goodnight
and see them to their car.
Don't leave yet,
we'll do another cigarette,
some wine.
Let's talk a little while
before you go.'*

*'Hey,
do you want me to turn
the music on?'*

December 2002

still three o'clock (franky's not at home)

franky's not at home
he's gone away and left an empty place
a timepiece on the mantle says
it's three o'clock
it said the same thing yesterday
and since the day it stopped
perhaps it's always going to be three o'clock

franky's gone away
please leave your message
slide it through the door
he's sure to find the envelope
when he comes home
pick it up and know the writing
turn it round and around
then put it on the mantle until three-o-one

franky's not at home it seems he's gone away
just said one day that he was packing bags
to leave
if there's a forward address he didn't think
to say
just something about the need to go
something about some things that he said
he didn't know
he had to leave
then he was gone

franky's not at home today
the silence on the mantle shelf
still reads that it's three o'clock

October 2002

storm bringer

I will hold my hands up to the sky
I will glare
the summons
clouds are gathering
a swirl above my head

I will call out *ky-ay-ay-a-ay*
encircle
with powders
hear the voices call
rumble
they will come

I will disrobe in the windsongs cry
stand naked
feel the bite
in air of water
wet me
let it fall

they will rain
I will dance
splash moisture
on the ground
underneath my feet
upon my face

ky-ay-ay-a-ay

February 2003

stormy weather

Stormy days. The weather.
It's raining again.
It looks like more rain.
I can't see the road
There's rain in my eyes.
How long will it rain?
Where is the sun?

Clouded skies. Forever.
These days just drag on.
Must it rain for so long?
Hard to stand on the road,
It's raining so hard.
The skies are all wrong.
Where is the sun?

sweat dribble down

I had a sweat-dribble down my chin
when I frowned at the sun
the heat doesn't care
it's on a down hill

running over my face
around the corner of my eyes
I'm cursing at the blue
with a spit-choke mouth
like the rag red end
of a lung gone bad
from smoking so much
it never had a chance
and the day is just a cough along
in that way too

on a trickle running down
that got out and got away drop
by drop to the ground
till I'm low in my supply of flowing
essential fluids and I know for sure
that the heat doesn't care
but it started on a downhill
run from the moment that I frowned

April 2001

the fluent pen

The sometime fluent pen.
My sometime fluent pen.
Your sometime flowing body
My sometime lucid mind
Sometimes in my midnight I,
sometimes, reach my hand
(Your sometime sleeping body)
I sometimes never sleeping
I sometimes wakeful lying
I sometimes seek distraction
You are sometimes long away
You are sometimes out of reach
You sometimes hardly notice!
You sometimes hardly notice!

I sometimes do not speak of it
I, sometimes, do not say
But sometimes, in the night time
Sometimes in the night
I sometimes, sometimes, need you
Sometimes, sometimes, want you.
I sometimes cannot speak
So, my sometime fluent pen
Must somehow take the blame
For the sometimes in my lifetime
For the sometimes, every night
When I somehow have to write it
Else somehow go insane
So that somehow I can right it
Somehow, sometime, again.

The Kiss

Published in The Lakes and Longbeach Gazette, June 2000 edition.

A kiss
Being what it is
Was irresponsible!
But the thought
Rolling round my head
Was irresistible!
My lips
Once upon their way
Were irreversible!
Your taste
Devouring all my senses
So irrepressible!
To kiss you, time and time again -
Extreme delight.

A kiss is irresistible
Being what it is
My thoughts so irrepressible
From rolling round my head
My irresponsible lips
Are on their way!
My senses, irreversible
Devour your taste
Extreme delight to kiss you
Time and time again.

July 1998

the messenger

well
I can tell you
it was unnerving

you could hear him approaching
from a long way off
not loud
but a kind of murmuring voice

nothing remarkable about the way he looked
just blue-check flannel shirt
some outdoors pants and boots
a hat of some sort
for the sun
set back on his head
I could see his face quite clearly

look
there wasn't anything in particular
about the face either
a fairly ordinary looking character
you'd say
brown eyes I think
shaved within the last day or so
not looking at anything in particular
no mood I could identify

it may have been his gait
that set me off first
it was a kind of aimless unrelenting plod
that at the same time seemed purposeful
as though it was aimless for a reason
deliberate
if you understand me

it's difficult I know
I'm not explaining well
his arms seemed stiff at his sides
as he moved

there was just something about him

he was singing
looking out into the air and singing
not quite under his breath
and without putting his mind to it

I could hear it eventually

you'll come running back
you'll come running back to me

and then a sucking whistle
out of time and out of tune

I was near frozen in place by this time
I can't tell you why
just the feeling of something
about to happen
as he walked past me
he turned and looked me full in the face
and he grinned and said
he didn't sing it
he said

time is on my side

as though it was a message
intended for me personally
and it meant something

I just turned and ran inside
locked the door behind me
and leaned up against the wall
I was gasping for such a long time

oh
he gave me such a turn

look at me
I'm still shaking

April 2003

the negative weight of craters on the face of the moon

today I will write for you
I will tell you of a man
who sought to cup the stars
in the palms of his hands
like so many dreaming men before him
but was bent beneath a burden
of the weight of craters

there will be a short stanza
about his clamber-crawl
from troubled emptiness

a line about the way he found release

reference to the opening
of eyes
a fleeting glimpse of beauty
that almost brought him to his knees again

and something of the unconscious opening
of his arms
reaching to make a cradle
seeking the warmth of an embrace

some words about a falter
for only a moment
and then the vision gone
but for the moon
so round and white
hung low and draped in heaviness
shadows showing faintly
the pock-marks and scars
that were all that he could hold

I will share with you the story
of a void reached by a man
who at one time strove
to touch each and every star

Frank Prem

I will talk about the velocity
of dreams
that fall to earth
and of the unseen weight contained within
the colour-blue of the craters of the moon

today when I am ready
I will write

October 2002

the old familiar

it is an old familiar
a feeling that emerges suddenly
without identifying itself
or the reasons for emergence at that time

I recall once
it struck in mid-sentence
causing a blush and a stammer
a quick excuse to leave
and then a dementia of confusion

and here it is again
maybe

eye contact is good
conversation is buoyant
opinions are relatively common ground
the passage of time
is extended
unnoticed

the mind games have started
about the meaning in a look
genuine interest or politeness
to risk a touch or no touch
by hand or by leg
accident or intent
not this time
maybe next
maybe never

and afterwards thinking
what was that all about
if I . . .
maybe . . .
when . . .

no

well
maybe yes

yes
it's that old familiar
of excitement
fear and tension
hungry anticipation

and it's back

April 2003

the reviewer

why relief
he asked himself

it wasn't better
sometimes worse
always
always
less

so why the feeling of relief

like a third person
a reviewer
hovering above
he looked back and down
at himself

how good it had been

how hard he found it to speak
what was in his head
to say it aloud
as though the sound of the words
would turn everything into overblown reality
or prove the falsehood

every good thing magnified
to impossible goodness

every negative grown large
to loom insurmountable

how the unspoken could be ignored
changed if need be
or hugged in a warmth
that had never been aspired to
could never be uttered aloud
for fear

he looked at her
how she needed
to hear him

his thoughts

his feelings

his reassurance

how he had tried sometimes
to give her what she had needed

the way it made him sweat
shake in discomfort
like a confrontation
with the unformed part of himself

so much angst
for what was
really
so very little

but beyond
what he could find

he looked again
at the incomplete
mental tally

the good things

the deficiencies

his capacity to change

the likelihood now
of ever needing to

this relief is an unsatisfying form
but review
remains an internal process
ongoing

February 2003

the ride

One trip for new adventure
One stride upon the road
One step along, for the bravehearts
One stumble (overload).

One leap towards tomorrow
One walk to the sunny side
One turn to banish shadows
Once more, forward-ho, the ride.

February 1999

the spread

the modern house is laid out
in a sensible design pattern
for example the entry
fronts the kitchen
where food preparation is a pleasure
on imported italian benches
designer stove and cupboards
the dishwasher is active but is silent

while adjoining is a dining room
round table and four chairs
for cosy little gatherings
or family meals taken in the evening
between children's shows and news time
on the tv in the corner

it's pleasant
snug and nice

there is a lounge room
with a space for entertainment
a nook to make a library
and excellent separation
of the ensuite and master bedroom
from the number two and three neat bedrooms
the laundry and a bathroom

it all fits together well
ideal for the modern family
not too large for them
no no

~

I rattle around this house
in the middle of suburbia
it's a long way from my office
in a spare bedroom
through the kitchen
past the lounge and to my bedroom

I leave the television on up there
so I can hear the sound of something
other than my echo and the clatter
of my fingers pounding at the keyboard
the quiet can disconcert me
but not even the neighbours can hear me
when I shout to hear my voice sound out
the fence-line is designed to maximise my privacy

the spare room is kept at ready
for a visit from somebody
I don't know who or when or why
but if they come I know it will be ready

the dining room is a storage space
the table is surrounded almost covered up
in papers from this job or that
and the kitchen bench
holds a week of mail and three local papers
it's almost always bills and the papers
get redirected to the garbage can

I do the dishes once a while
it's hard to justify the dishwasher and I am loath
to wash by hand
I don't dirty them too often I don't cook
except the electric fry-pan
on top of the fancy griller of the stove
to fry an egg
from time to time

it's a good job that I like my space uncluttered
I have always travelled lightly on possessions
and I have an acreage of house now to myself
like an indoor farmer I can roam
the paddocks of my own open range
yee ha yee ha

I better go check the boundaries

April 2003

time to dance

you've turned the music on
captain fantastic

you and I know all the words
every song is a familiar
I know when you turn it on
you want to dance

your husband has gone to bed
we have drunk cab sav
and merlot wine
talked until it's late
and I believe it is time
I should be going

but when you turn the music on
I understand I mustn't leave
now has come the mood
you need to dance

we will make our judgments
about volume
when he opens the bedroom door
sleep-squinting
to wave that we are loud

then you will teach me
once again
the way to twirl you
on the floor
cheek to cheek and back to back
until the night turns into early

rocking side by side
we'll close our eyes to sing
full voice and open heart
we will move together
captain fantastic and his sidekicks
after your husband has gone to bed
we will sing
you and I will dance

November 2002

to make it worthwhile

he said

> I leave the book out on my coffee table
> so anyone can take a look
> sort of an encouragement -
> a conversation starter
> a lot of the women I know are either models
> or painters
> and they like checking out the images
> commenting on the poses and postures
> the aesthetics of it

she said

> for you men
> it's all about the visuals   the pictures
> show a man a picture of a nude woman
> and he's off
> halfway to being satisfied already
> it isn't the same for a woman
> show me a picture of a naked man or woman
> and I'll say
> oh yes very nice and then move on
> I'll tell you what a woman likes
> she likes to be engaged by the eyes
> by touch
> and by the tone of a man's voice

he said

> I'm seeing three women at the moment

adding

> it's all above board
> they all know about each other
> but it isn't the same as when I was in love
> it's a little empty
> love is a kind of 'value-add' to sex
> but it isn't critical
> and the girls are all lovely
>
> I'm honest with them
> I don't tell them I'm a good man
> or any bullshit like that
> no promises

she said

> there comes a point
> where a woman can do without the sex
> and will choose to
> when you've known a few men
> in your life
> sex is not the primary thing
> there has to be more than that
> if there isn't the intimacy of love
> even if only fleeting
> why bother going through the motions
> there comes a point
> where it needs to be a celebration
> to be worth the bother
>
> for a woman

she said

> there has to be more
> to make it worthwhile

April 2003

tonight blues

think I'll play
blues tonight
want a woman with a wail
and a husky husky voice
to tell me
this is the only way

think I better play dark blues tonight
hear somebody
tell me about a hard day
in a hard life
low-down guitar
and harmonica to howl

    wa-wa-wa-wa
    wa-wa-wa-wa

I hear them calling
think I must have
some blues
tonight

October 2002

watchful credit

I can't escape the feeling that my credit card
is watching me
every month it knows the places
that I've been
details of the way I blow my pay packet
a tracking of my life that empties me
of secrets

I am assured discretion
I am told that no one knows
but

by definition I thought statements
must be spoken loud
at least the writing ought to be in bold
but these numbers shown in warming red
are hard to see
without my glasses full of spirit
sometimes I can't believe the items
reassembled from a month or more ago
I'm quite convinced they must be watching me

in their discretion
confidentially ensuring
someone knows

June 2001

wedding song

On floating lace
And penguins tails
A ship all new
S'lightly sails

To unknown waters
And sleeping pools
The helmsman steers them
Beyond the fools

That reach from lands
Gone grey with age
Who'd invite them in
To rest a stage.

But penguin tails
And flashing lace
Sail by as though
They're in a race.

They tack away
Or run the breeze
To chart new oceans
Or drift at ease.

They float together
The two entwined
The penguin, the lace
On their ship aligned.

Now gone away
To distant place
With a wake of tail
And a flash of lace.

1998 (earlier)

whispered voice (over and over)

whispered voice
floating over traffic noise
I can hear it call
over me and over

heavy air
filter down to ease despair
I can feel the comfort fall
over me and over

everyone that takes a step
on this sidewalk of uncertainty knows
the touch of loneliness among
the cracked and broken crowds
that move in stealth and silently come
over me and over

a peaceful sound
that only my mind has found
rising up above it all
over me and over

March 2001

The Golub Suite

#1 - pigeon-trification

it should be no surprise that it might take
some time
for we have lived here awhile now
and locating the café latte set
has proven difficult
only the over-crowded shopping malls
cater for such needs
while quiet streets appear uninitiated
so no
it should not be a great surprise
but there is hope

all through this morning we have watched
the patient industry
of two diamond-necked pigeons
at the task of home building
sitting quietly on the fence at first light
they seemed a pair of fat puffballs
but with the day they have emerged

to gather precisely shaped twigs and grasses
placed just so

to settle down leaves until a platform
is achieved
no sharp protuberances

busy busy

and with the day now well advanced
and home made comfortable
these young residents
of an unsophisticated suburbia
must confront a test

to be approached obliquely
as though still nonchalantly seeking twigs
although there is no evidence
of continued purpose in this regard

to be examined with a suspicious eye
although appearances seem inviting enough

to be sampled sparingly at first
with a rapid extension of neck
and dart of beak
for the achievement of an initial taste

a patisserie has opened at the base of the tree
in which the new nest has been established
and french cuisine provided
so while other birds may have bread crumbs
in the aging feeder
this domicile is going up-market
and while it has taken a little time
habit-formation has begun

croissant flakes anyone?

September 2002

#2 - homemaking in adverse conditions

the golub couple have taken up residence
two days ago they built a nest
hidden inside the shrubs and growth
that mark the back fence
a day of twiggery and toil
then it was done

yesterday the wind blew loud all day
the outside world was gusted movement
and twitching restlessness all night
no sign of the golubs to be seen
only the wind

but this morning in the lull they are there
mister is sitting quiet on a branch
fluffed and ruffled but stalwart in his posture
looks hardly more than a chick
but he's set himself to do the tasks
of a bigger bird
mrs golub is seated in shelter on the nest
almost invisible with just her head moving
she appears from time to time
behind the patience of his shoulder

it may take more than weather and wind
to discourage these new neighbours of ours

September 2002

#3 - interior decoration

her tail is up
white feather-down
beneath the purple-dun shading
of her upper body
she is working her way
through three hundred and sixty degrees
to settle the materials into a shape
that suits her contours

he is on the ground
selecting yet another stem of dry grass
this one forks towards the tapered end
considering carefully weight and balance
before attempting force
to maneuver through the shrubbery
for deposit and inspection

she works her way
again
through three hundred and sixty degrees

September 2002

#4 - identifying the golubs

well the golubs seem just the same
as all the rest of them if you ask me
put them in a crowd and I can't tell
one from another

they've all got a diamond studded collar
adorning the back of their necks
and that purple-brown colour
they all walk the same and sound the same

it's because they live outside
my kitchen window
that I know they're my pair
and not just any coo-cooing pigeons
it's only then that I know who they are

they all look the same to me

September 2002

#5 - unceasing vigilance

they always seem aware of when I stand
at the window
watching them at their daily business

they don't stop what they are doing
so perhaps they are accustomed or conditioned
lulled into believing all is safe
they may be right
although there can be no guarantees
I may only be benign while behind brick walls
and glass windows
and there are greater forces at work
even than those that I represent

but how is it they are so aware

I have not seen or heard
that they have great eyesight
watchful certainly but not particularly noted
hearing should not be a factor
possibly in the new age paranoia has spread
even to such as these residents
of the shrubs outside my window

or perhaps it is merely the impression
of eternal watchfulness
that comes from location of eyes
at the side of the head

September 2002

#6 - premature flight

I am standing below the nest
where she has laid

tense now
unused to so close a presence as mine
very still
only her eyes follow my movements
perhaps she will sit it out
courage in the face of the unknown
perhaps

the sound of wings is sudden
loud as a gunshot
she has flown
in the end I was so near
she could not bear it

I too am unsuited for such closeness
and must leave

September 2002

The New West

the new west: a touch of succulence on barkly street

this would have to be Footscray
where else to find
the Melbourne Chinese Bible Church
but on Barkly Street

a launderette
an empty ex-Vietnamese eatery
and a combination flower shop
and coffee parlour
of deep blue looks
that might have been transplanted
from a place altogether more salubrious
as suggested by the decorative lounge setting
and specimens of local intelligentsia
absorbed in gazette gossip
surrounded as they sit by bouquets
in tin buckets
and the smell of incense burning so fragrantly
that interloper I
am driven out onto the street
like an ill-tolerated
and poorly reconstructed gauche
to sit at varnished plywood on the footpath
atop a lumpen sixties-vinyl kitchen chair
forced to assume a straight back
like a child at a school desk

there are identical parasols visible
through the window
seen behind a reflection off the glass frontage
they seem pretty delicacies
perhaps Chinese
but more likely the Footscray Market
on Saturday

my table boasts an electroplated teapot
anchored safely in the embrace
of an unused ashtray
it is a lushness this pouring device
succulents grope from the spout
and protrude from beneath the lid
a small touch of *florist-on-the-footpath*
lest one forget
there is more than a single purpose here

Margarita's next door is closed
the hanging sign dates back to my childhood
she sold children's wear and gifts once

April 2002

the new west: main street west

Main Street West crosses the railway line
then heads up past the high school

as a child the path we took
to visit my city cousin
ended on this stretch of road
turning right when we passed the school
then meandering through avenues
parades and ways
all unfamiliar concepts to a lad from the sticks
where naming conventions were plain
and my street was designated '*last*'
to signify the end of the bitumen
of civilisation
and the commencement of dirt tracks
and scrub

I recall a multicultural homogeneity
in the St. Albans (*Sunta Ahlbunz*)
of those days
Slavs and Greeks and Italians
Maltese Hungarians and Germans
a great mishmash of humanity
emerged from post-war central Europe
mingled and stirred
in the melting pot
of the outer western suburbs
working at Massey Ferguson to build tractors
at Ford to assemble cars
and at Rowntrees to pack chocolate biscuits

today I see the same European faces
on Main Street West
but they walk slowly
taking measured steps
and carrying smaller packages
with no children

they have aged forty years
passed from the vigour and promise
of new arrivals
with futures to build and homes to make
from being people with children to raise
and a new land to interpret and to control
into age pensioners with paunched stomachs
and combination dialects of mixed English
and mother tongue

they are passed as they walk
on Main Street West
by young people with vigour in their steps
and small children clustered
around the woman
while her man walks a step ahead
Asian eyes and straight black hair
Afghan skin and head-to-toe shawl
and dresses
sing-song voices and guttural drawls
that sound as though they belong here
and have a stake in the sunshine
that is playing across the footpath
and into shop windows
that spell *fine food* in Vietnamese

Main Street West has changed
but everything is still the same
I no longer turn right after the high school

April 2002

the new west: reverse parking at three thirty

there is a reason why it is referred to
as *Rafferty's Rules*
in the car park
women one after another are stopping
in the centre of the bitumen
then reverse parking to left or right
as though for a quick getaway

uninitiated
I park nose-to-kerb

a swarm of children
like ants or bees
in gaudy maroon tops and baggy shorts
or mock-tartan checked blue skirts
running and shouting

they are everywhere
throwing bulky bags to ground
as though inflicting a gleeful punishment
on objects not worthy of respect
or second thought

they
are the reason for strange practices
in the car park
these children in broad rimmed hats
that mark the sun as an enemy
and wearing loud colours
once unfamiliar in school precincts
for it is half past three in the afternoon
and the school day is ended

mothers know
that sensible people do not risk reversing
into the frenzied dispersal
of school children and cars
in the crazed quarter-hour
after school is dismissed
only passing strangers
would attempt such feats

March 2002

the new west: a ride on the st albans line

stifling heat and open windows
torn green-leather seats with stuffing removed
kids parked in the doorways
daringly keeping the doors open
leaning against one
holding feet against the other

heads protrude
from the swaying wooden carriages
quickly withdrawn
at the unsubtle approach of a steel pylon
too far away to do damage
too close not to flinch

lasting architectural impressions
of the nineteen seventies western suburbs
drawn from the fleet glimpses
of unkempt backyards
and squalid loading bays of shops
and small factories
that line the fringes of the tracks
there must be a rule
in town-planning guidebooks
that one 'Station Street' has to be assigned
to every suburb along the route

the inter-suburban 'red-rattler'
bullock-dances its way down the St Albans line
all change
this is the last stop
catch a bus if you want to go
to Sunbury

March 2002

the new west: community health in the new west

it is a strong attractive facade in cream brick
solid
authoritative and welcoming
it seems to make a statement

> *we are here for you*
> *we will care*
> *we are yours*
> *we will stay*

long outside walls are partially concealed
close-planted creepers and tall shrubs
a screen against close examination
but the inside is bouncing steps
on yielding floors
a carpet-coat to disguise imperfect joins
that cut across corridors
between abutted sections

sloping revelation confirms uneven floor levels
between pre-fabs #4 and #5

the footsteps and muffled speech
of fifty staff and assorted clients
rise and mingle in an invisible fog
a murmur and echo
that enters and occupies rooms 33 to 67

and sundry connecting spaces

the doors on these *permanent-temporaries*
have rigid aluminium frames and a handle
that is missing its keyhole
an external padlock-latch bolted at head height
has to suffice for security

The New West

a shed-like and ramshackle quality pervades
reminiscent of an object discarded
to a place always on the edge of sight
but never clearly in focus

cramped and functional toilets
no porcelain in sight
only a small trough of galvanised flat-iron
mounted halfway up the wall
an elbow-joint from the washbasin
and a thickness of particle-board away
from sound of a baby crying
in the mothers room next door

this is permanence
here in the New West

March 2002

the new west: new west

this is the west
the *new* west
a place of contrasts

old industry and aging housing
for the 50's immigrants
old Europe come in hope to live
in new Australia
to be '*New Australians*'

more recent is the stagnant slippage
into unemployment
boredom
drugs and suicide rates
urban leprosy and tawdry reputation

new housing tracts of five hundred homes
in a hit
welcome to beautiful Caroline Springs
just ten kilometres up the freeway from Melton
growth corridors sans infrastructure

new-wave arrivals

>*Vietnam*
>*Afghanistan*
>*Cambodia*

new support groups
and migrant resource centres
loneliness and depression

the *service-partnership* meeting
is peopled by community representatives
with old-European faces
the early immigrant waves
have become '*establishment*' here
there are no Asian faces
and only three men in a sea of women

The New West

Ms Urbana is in the chair
on behalf of the indigenously named
Community Health Centre
a tall big-boned woman with round face
and round eyes
dark hair touched with purple tones
reflected in the down-lights
she has no accent but that of Keilor
and yet she is straight out of some Slavia

Vesna is the admin assistant
Lydia has a point of order

the coordinator of projects has caught my eye
with the movement of her hands
her several rings catching the light
she also may be multi-faceted
the fingers are extraordinary   an over-sized slenderness

she is using the long pointer
to make a circle that remains
hanging in the air as an outline
the width of her fingertip
when she makes a fist for emphasis
it is the size of a man
a disproportionately powerful appearance
on such a slender body frame

this is the new west
old wogs in control
new wogs
the out-of-sight subjects of discussion

> *welcome aboard sir*
>
> *what do you have to contribute?*

March 2002

A Random Alphabetical

a bad week

the town was already old when I was young
had been through many iterations
from small pastoral
to boom-gold and bushranger
from public-service hub
to centre for visitors
who chose to spend their passing time
peering over relics
of the almost forgotten

home was perched
right on the beaten track
around the corner from an edifice
above the vantage for a view

strangers passed daily
drawn to catch a glimpse
to try to bridge
the distance in their minds
between then and now

on foot
in car
by bus
day-trippers all

for that was before the township awoke
before the profits of encouragement
by bed and by breakfast
were well understood
or the potential return
from organisation of diversions
had been calculated

we youthful anti-heroes
resentful ingrates that we were
thought them invaders of private ground
to be made uncomfortable if possible

often I have thought of visiting Bali
was envious of friends that went
but opportunity seemed never to arise
I don't feel the same way now
and probably I will not visit

once my destiny seemed university
to be a teacher of some subject related to words
and to writing them prettily
it will not happen now

yesterday a classroom was painted
handgun red
for the second time in a year or so
these are no conditions
for a love of words
and I am grown so very much older

my chosen path turned to mental health
where so many people do what they can
using themselves to make a change
to help straighten out distorted thinking
but last week a woman I knew
was slain outside an elevator door
a few steps back from lunch
nobody knows for sure
why she was the chosen one
but they put her below ground
just yesterday
and I don't enjoy my work
the way I used to
when I was young
and the town was old

we didn't like our visitors
very much
we thought them rubber-necks
poking over things rightfully ours
collectively we named them *terrorists*
not *tourists*
and wished them away to other places

A Random Alphabetical

this has been a bad week
but I swear
we meant no malice

October 2002

a circlet of pearls

I wear a circlet of black pearls
in a necklace
it is not a matter of fashion or style
for I have no consciousness of such things
I keep them covered by shirt and collar
these baubles of mine

organic trinkets
they grow and I watch them changing
shape and size and hue
becoming darker and larger

today with fire
and red anger splayed across my skin
a new one has erupted into existence

I will watch in the days to come
as the anger dies and the red fades
my new pearl will darken
and emerge

I wear a circlet of pearls in a necklace
dark

they grow

August 2001

a contact for astro-man

he's like an astro-man
at the wireless
sending messages into the sky
waiting for a contact
from far away
in places he has never been
but *believes in*
with a fervour
like religion

a kind of mania
that drives him every night
even when the sounds
start out with the

    oooo-eeee-oooo

that hints there'll be nothing out there
this time

he keeps turning dials
and sending
heart-felt messages

once he thought he had an interaction
with a shooting star
but it passed right through his signal range
so quickly
that now he wonders
if it was real
and this time he's hoping
for a pulsar
that might hear him
and send a signal back
to say hello in static
or thrum a rhythmic beat
that will let him know for sure
he is not alone
in the universe

an astro-man
a pedant if you start him up
because he still believes
there'll be a signal out there one day
tuned in to his frequency

if he only searches hard enough
and patiently
there will be a contact
from way out in the great nowhere

someone will hear him

April 2003

a wicked man (just trust me)

I'm a wicked, wicked, man
But if you let me take your hand
(you can trust me).

I see, from where I stand
That you're uncertain, but. . .
(you can trust me).

I didn't figure in your plans
But baby, they were bland
Come on (and trust me).

Don't think you understand
We're talking something grand
(if you just trust me).

I'm as wicked as can be
You'll like it, wait and see
(and trust me).

Take your doubts and let them be
Just do what fate decreed
Mmmm (trust me).

Trust me

Trussssssst me

Oh, you can trust me

Just tru....

January 1999

an absentee; a companion

and it comes at last
in these middle years
even to me

tempestuousness it seems
passes with youth
until a point

you searched for it long ago
but I was hungry
driven
moving at pace
ravenous

my analysis
yes I was *the analyst* even then
my analysis knew
that you longed for affection
for evidence of that soft emotion
while I sought
what I believed were the great intimacies
physical knowledge
too soon then for me
to pursue the gentle sport
of peace of mind

perhaps that's the nature of youth
pursuit of the unattainable
simplistic complexity
until another day spent alone
wondering who's to be called
to break the surrounding silence
and a realisation
that affection
is a desirable absentee

regret
an abiding companion

A Random Alphabetical

I remember though
what you wanted
know that I have arrived there
in these middle years
such a long way
behind you

attraction (by the bottle)

but that's the thing about attraction
isn't it
it's not like two magnets
one minute you're chatting away
good friends no complications
the next
a look in the eyes
a change in the air
something happens l

look around you
nothing to see that's different
look at her and it's . . .
awkward
try to resist
and it makes no difference
pulled forward
closer

then you're touching
lips to lips
maybe a hand brushing the face
a leg making contact
and electricity

you might wonder
what was that
what just happened

doesn't matter
you can't turn it back
or turn it off

attraction
wouldn't you just love
to bottle it

calling late

Do you mind me calling you late?
No.
No?
No.

That's good,
well, that's great.
I couldn't wait
to get you on the phone,
just to check
if you're still alone?
Yes. Yes?
Yes.
Yes, I can hear the silence
on your bed, as you are speaking.
Glad to know,
with me not there,
there's no-one sneaking
in to my place.

And do you miss me?
Say yes.
Do you want me home?
Say yes.
Do you need my touch?
Say yes,
yes, yes, yes.

I'll be back soon. Stay alone
until I roll up to your door.
Then let me in,
to set to working,
make you cry for more, more,
more, more.
Do you mind me calling late?
No.

No?
No.

cloudy face prayer

lord this is earth
I am alone too far from
water-blue we look
from where you gaze on us

we are that colour
not only sky above
but there's a sea somewhere
that's running too

I watch to try to see you
in between
the picture-faces made by clouds
they're only distorted scenes
only suggestions
if I turn my head
I cannot find you there

perhaps in water
underneath the ocean swirl
I hold my breath and open eyes
once to glimpse
a gliding ray

was it you

do you watch from there
the things that happen
past the break
of surf on land
or in the atmosphere surrounding earth

and lord
I am alone
too far from water blue
look down on me once
if you will
show me a cloudy face

comfort movies

he calls them comfort flicks
video tapes
for the VCR

movies made
back in the golden days
of contract stars and starlets
sausage-factory produced scenarios
for the leads

mitchum and taylor
and bogart
bacall and hepburn
and hepburn and tracey
wayne and bronson
monroe

romance and adventure
the wild west
and atticus finch
sirens and seductions

comfort flicks
predictable and sure
familiar

he hires them on monday
for a week
for the nights
when television is a desert
and a wasteland of hours
stretches ahead
interminable
intolerable

for when the gaps
are too hard to fill
and being alone
is just one reel
too many

damp spirits

this is not the way I saw
life unfolding when I was small
when every dream was waiting for
a dreamer

days seemed to dance ahead
calling out for one more step
fresh colours from the palette
of the painter

I was only running
the way that young ones run
trying to find a path to lead me
around corners
sun was always fire and heat
when I tried to touch the sky
but
reaching up was the only way
that I knew

now it's another ace for solitaire
and one more evening gone
there's nothing like monotony
for thinkers

hours that stretch the night ahead
fill up with the radio
ancient airs rewound to taunt
a bad singer

I wouldn't really call this running
more like a slow retreat
no eagerness for stealing looks
around corners

reaching up to touch the sky
now means just another drop of rain
nothing dilutes the spirit
like water

A Random Alphabetical

I wouldn't call it running
just a slow retreat
that feels the same
as falling down
like water

April 2000

expression of interest sought (apply within)

wanted
is a woman's touch
in a place that's showing signs
of falling into age
and disrepair

certain rooms
are in need of dusting and a tidy-up
to make them shine again

the fluttery of subtle webs
in each suggested breeze
is unattractive
indicating that too long has passed
without an intervention
and requiring remedial activity
as a matter of some urgency

the owner
a bachelor of good intent
whose execution lets him down
is seeking now
for expressions of interest
from applicants of quality
who will pay due attention
to the detailed ministration
of a woman's touch
to those areas identified
as most in need
of rejuvenation

apply within

January 2003

enclosed by cloud

cloud across the bay
is swallowing stars

a wave of incoming tide
is following, dark
like a heart spinning unwound
and fading away

i am drinking shadows
from a glass

the wine of bleeding red
was meant to last
until the bitter taste was gone
but i'll take it now

the gaze i cast towards you was me
naked and exposed

the toast i raised to salute you
was a dream

i am blind and the drink is spilled
across the way
that it might have been

only the dregs
are what they seemed

the cloud above my head
has swallowed my stars
and the following dark
is enclosing me

October 2000

flying home

hello
it's me
i'm up here in the sky
flying just below the white-cloud
canopy of god non-stop from brisbane
south to melbourne
and i'm holding onto my breath from now
until i get back home

i've been away a moment
but it feels so long
the days have been a haze
of sun and sand and water
and the dance we had in a city mall
to entertain five restaurants
that we didn't think
were watching us

the waves have broken on my body
washed me clean like an abrasion
from the surf that threw me
into sand with violence unpremeditated
just a casual fling
that took on meaning
through days of constant aching

hey
i'm flying now
above the canopy of god
going home and holding breath
to see what's changed
if it's all the same
i might have turned brown and blue
for nothing

September 2000

fuck you fever poem

I remember when I wrote it
I read it and revised
line by line
tried to cast my thoughts back
to the very moment
so I could recall it perfectly
write it down
just the way it rewound
in my mind

I made the words
flow across the page
capturing my heat
in drawn analogies
to show the turmoil
as I was on my way
to falling

I dressed them
in small curlicues and flourishes
carefully in a frame
gave them
like a bond
so like a vow
falling in love I was
feverish

~

I found the fever poem today
face down on the table
where I had recycled
an old frame
for a *'bless this house'*

wrapped up to give away
and on the bench there it was
the fever piece
returned
as I recall

amid a few old shirts
that no longer fit me
and a 'fuck you'

~

neither sorry nor goodbye
just a 'fuck you' note
padded up with possibilities
and openings
for another time
and place

I didn't read it today
just held it a short time
while I looked away at someplace else
then crumpled it
into the garbage bag

now I guess
there's just one more thing
I need to do
to finally end
this love affair

January 2003

I am the place

I am the secret
hidden in the deep
of your mind.

I am the light
dancing pleasure
in your eyes.

I am the mystery
held in the soft curve
of your smile.

I am the web
woven by the beating
of your heart.

I am the cloak
masking thoughts
inclined to stray.

I am the place
for refuge and retreat
of safe haven.

I am your place.

April 1999

Frank Prem

I might move closer

Poem of the Week (4/11/02) at Wild Poetry Forum

in another time another place
I would do differently
I might look around the room
for orientation
move my body
beneath the shape of sheet and blanket
to feel warmth all over
roll to the side
gaze for a moment
move closer
make contact
close my eyes again

it's almost six o'clock in the morning

I will rise
trek to the shop for coffee and the paper
let cold breeze caress my face
before the sun peers
above the rooftops
a shiver and a cigarette
are an early start to a long day

but in another place and time
I might move closer

October 2002

kiss me

Kiss me in the morning
Kiss me once or twice
Kiss me very quickly
Kiss me . . . very nice.

Kiss me in the lunchtime
Kiss me there . . . and there
Kiss me at your leisure
Kiss me if you dare.

Kiss me in the evening
Kiss me through the night
Kiss me very slowly
Kiss me . . . yes . . . that's right.

Kiss me when you're waking
Kiss me, kiss me in your sleep
Kiss me when you want me
Kiss me, kiss me deep.

November 1998

like almonds

> *October 10 2002 is/was National Poetry Day in the UK.*
> *Poets were asked to write on the theme of 'Celebration'.*
> *I have been searching for thoughts and phrases to string together a verse*
> *or two for poetry day but I have parted from my muse.*

and the words come out clumsy and flat
not forming stories that flow
but leave me floundering
with three lines of bullshit
about believing
about faith
the difference between the two
and . . .

erase them from the screen
try again later

today I selected some pieces to read
at a poetry gig that is new to me
I searched the collected archive
and found nothing new
only dancing words formed in another life
now seemingly ended

a young man approached me
asked if I had published the pieces he'd heard
could I send them to him
for his magazine
any one of the three would be fine

I wrote them for her
I wrote them about her
no
they haven't appeared anywhere else

a month ago
I would see reason to celebrate
and in truth I am happy even now
yes I am

but the aftertaste
is bitter
like a lingering odour
of almonds

I will send them to him
they are no further use to me

October 2002

liquor song

Hold that sweet bottle
Hold it close, to your lips
Smell the sweet liquor
Taste it . . . little sips.

Catch the hot feeling
Roll it, on your tongue
Bathe in heat intentions
Taste it . . . liquor song.

Close your eager eyes
Take, a larger swallow
Drink it to the limit
Taste it . . . more to follow.

Mmm, love that sweetest bottle
Holds taste, as good as this
Drink with free abandon
Taste it . . . liquor kiss.

October 1998

little boy blue

Little boy blue
Come play on the path
Sit down beside me
And let's hear you laugh

Laugh at the ant trails
Laugh at the bees
Laugh darling little boy
At all that you see.

With little boy logic
Explain all the fates
To your faithful old teddy
Who patiently waits

My small little boy
My growing young man
You'll soon up and away
As only little boys can.

July 1998

maybe elvis

With hindsight, I can see that we were foolish,
but it was easy to get swept up
by the moment,
and to believe.

Looking back of course, it's easy to work out,
but I was there when it happened
and there was nothing anyone could do
but go along,
and for a moment,
to believe.

Somebody shouted out, 'It's Elvis!'
A hundred eyes were turned
to the sound.
Almost everybody knows that Elvis
is gone,
but we all turned,
and more than one of us believed,
for just a moment,
maybe it was Elvis.

I know that we were, all of us, quite foolish.
It only took a moment in the crowd.
I suppose that there are lessons
to be learned
about payment of attention,
but for a moment I believed
I saw a sequin flash and disappear
inside 'Aladdin's Cave',
just behind a knick knack shelf,
in a fast moving hint
that
maybe
I saw Elvis.

June 2000

A Random Alphabetical

mis-arrangement of flowers

there were roses in the bottom
of a rubbish bin on Main Street
down in Chelsea
the wrapping paper informs me
they'd never been inside a vase

as I was butting out a cigarette
on the metal-edge of the bin I wondered
why they were discarded
still tightly rolled in shades of apricot
among the tattered paper bags
and empty drink containers

but no-one else had noticed
and I know I shouldn't be surprised
nobody looks for roses
in the rubbish containers on Main Street
down in Chelsea

maybe the only ones who know
are somebody with a heart that's aching
and another who is trying to ignore
the staring crystal-whiteness
of an empty vase

July 2001

mystery and tedium

are we not

she said

all
thrilled with mystery
do we not desire those de-
licious moments
not
knowing
precisely
what is happening
don't you
find it maddening the need
to know

and isn't it extraordinary when
there's something new
you simply must ex-
plore

doesn't it keep you
on your toes
doesn't it make you
choose your clothes more carefully
put on make up
get the hair done so
organise to have a ...

but how boring

she said

A Random Alphabetical

when there's no-
thing hidden
nothing left for you to un-
cover
for the betterment
and good
of your soul
don't you feel
the need
for a little dis-
tance
some room to breathe in

as the air
gets heavy
draped around you
it cloys fam-
iliar to you it is
too
too
old

oh doesn't it get tedious
when it's all

so . . .

known

February 2003

nearly love

i lie in my bed
the dark
enfolds and surrounds me
the lady is there
yet miles away
tonight is a gulf
between planets
it seems as if she doesn't care
i try
but without effort
we live each end of a great vacuum
between us
some bottle-necked junction
we drift around
and drift around
sometimes i just want to break out
be off
away
to run and run
but then
i cant summon energy
i sap it all
in drifting around
a prisoner
in the great black hole
of nearly love

July 1999

no telling

Well, he said:

> *Tell me.*

But I said:

> *Trust me*
> *you, don't want to know.*

He said:

> *No, I mean it, tell me.*
> *I want to know.*

I said:

> *I really don't think you do.*

He said:

> *Yes I do,*
> *quit holding back.*
> *What kind of a mate are you?*

I said:

> *Are you sure?*
> *I mean,*
> *don't come back at me later*
> *and say I shouldn't have told you.*

He said:

No, no,
I really want to know.
I need to hear it.

So then, I said:

All right,
if that's what you want.

And so I told him

Well,
you should have seen it.
Tore his guts out, it did,
like I knew it would.
I tried to tell him not to,
but he wouldn't have it

Made me cough it up.

He shouldn't have made me do it,
but, you know
there's no telling
some people.

over lunch

Before lunch, I'll greet you at the door
We'll say our 'How do you do's'
Before lunch, we'll meet in sublime surrounds
I'll suggest that you may choose

Over lunch, we'll dine on fabulous fare
A little wine won't hurt
Over lunch, we'll satisfy those needs
And you may buy dessert.

During lunch, we'll speak of many things
We will dine and sip, at leisure
During lunch we'll speak our important pursuits
Like work, football, and pleasure.

After lunch, we'll relax in a comfortable state
This fresh young wine is so pert!
After lunch, you'll muse on the menu again
For you will buy dessert.

Having lunched, it is time to move along
Time to consider, where to?
Having lunched, there's a little place I know
I think it just right for we two.

Lets lunch, shall we do it all again?
Shall we act, fresh need to avert?
Lets lunch, I feel the pang of hunger now
Deign to be my dessert?

scotch sleeping

I scotch myself to sleep at night
I drink it till the bottles done
It's cheap and nasty, like my dreams
Tastes bitter on my tongue.

> *There's little pleasure in a bottle of scotch*
> *It isn't there to help me have fun*
> *And there's not much joy in whisky sleep*
> *But it's better than getting none.*

I fill my time in empty ways
In the dark, the reclusive one
Light of day brings memories back
Reminder that I made you run.

> *Can't bear the image that daylight brings*
> *A picture with you as the sun*
> *Seeing you, just seeing you*
> *Through the day I think of my gun.*

I smoke myself to an ashen mess
I smoke till there are no more
The blue grey haze dances and swirls
Then filters out the door.

> *There's no great promise in a tobacco pack*
> *It isn't there to slow my fall*
> *And there's not much hope in a cigarette life*
> *But it's better than no hope at all.*

I tell myself, what's done is done
I talk till I close my eyes
And when you appear, I talk to you
I still tell you those awful lies.

A Random Alphabetical

I speak the words that I just made up
Not truth - merest alibis
I'm saying things, just saying things
Through the night my failings reprise.

I Java myself, awake with the dawn
Black coffee to clear my head
It's hot and dark, like my fevered mind
Strong - it could wake the dead.

There's no jolly laughter in a Java jar
It can't hear the jokes I tell
And there's no new chuckles in a freshly brewed
But at least I ain't crying as well.

September 1998

ten signs of life

1 Impatiently

i can wait
until i see you
wait
until you're here
i can fill the time it takes
with easy memories

i can wait
but so impatiently
~

2 Flower Jug

flowers are filling a water jug
on the crowded table
that usually overflows
with mail and papers

i'm being forced
to make changes
and reconsider priorities

tomorrow i may buy a vase
~

3 Guitar

your guitar
is leaning on my sofa
it sounded to your strumming yesterday

i could pick it up
and run my fingers through the strings
to make a sound
but it needs your touch to make it play

~

4 Communal Earrings

with one
in your ear
and one that i rescued
lying here on the palm of my hand
these earrings
are acquiring communal properties

~

5 Elemental Air

it seems odd
that I've always believed the air
to be an elemental thing
containing the perfect combination
of gases and particles
to sustain a life
yet sharing your breath
appears to add so much value

~

6 New Sounds

this room has witnessed cheerful moments
and sadness staring at its walls

there have been tears sometimes
and there is trace evidence
of melancholy emptiness

I can't recall the last time
it was so startled
by the sounds
of giggling laughter

~

7 Rule Breaking

this sounds strange and foolish
but looking forward to seeing you
is breaking a personal rule

that alone is enough to keep me
lying awake at nights
pondering

~

8 Features

I seem to find similarities
to the features of your face
in greater or lesser part
in the faces of women
that I pass on the streets
in your absence

it improves their beauty

~

9 Snug Confusion

I am so reminded
of the days when my children were small
tucked snugly and tightly wrapped
inside their bedding
with just a glimpse of face peeping
for a kiss goodnight

sharing my bed with you
is a warm confusion

~

10 Basis for Goodbye

it grows wearisome
to be forever establishing a basis
for saying goodbye
from the point
of first hello

despite the fears
and the weaknesses
I despise in myself
it would be nice just one time
to stay

April 2000

solace

Up late,
and I'm running through my stuff, again.
I've been at it all day, since the crack of dawn,
working like a drone,
no moment of peace, just driven to go on.

And the numbers circling around my mind
are trickling through, like water.
Figures on the page
make no sense, something's out of order
and I'm thinking it's just me . . .

when she says,

Frankie,
are you coming to my bed?
Come on, Frankie,
I've got a place right here beside me.
Frankie bo-hoy,
the day is all but gone,
the night has come,
and I'm all alone.
Hey Frankie,
come in to keep me warm.

Hey Frankie,
come and make me warm.

~

Middle of the night,
think I must be sleeping.
I fell away somehow, in the pillow's song,
fallen too deep,
dreaming, the night is almost gone.

And the dreams that I dream
are thieves inside my slumber.
Images on a screen,
all slowed down in a crazy kind of wonder,
as they're calling out to me . . .

until she whispers,

Frankie,
are you really sleeping?
Come on, Frankie,
do you think you could hold on to me, now?
Frankie bo-hoy,
in the night that's left,
I need to feel your breath
warm up against my neck.

Hey Frankie,
take me in your arms.

Hey Frankie,
will you hold me in your arms?

November 1999

some dancing

I was ready
to go home
I'd said goodnight three times
but she said

> *one song*
> *let me teach you how to rock*
> *and roll*

so I twirled her round and round
and before I knew
we were dancing

to the left
to the right
change hands behind her back
shoulder up
and shoulder back
a little waltzing step for just four more bars
then I twirled her round
yes

we were dancing
long after I was ready
to go home

tango

I can't dance the tango
I am strictly still a watching man
who cannot dance to latin
but I saw that guy wiggle his behind
in a fancy little shuffle
while his girl almost popped out . . .
why is she hanging upside down
I swear she really almost popped out . . .

but did you see the way her leg flicked
right up among his articles
I didn't know to tango
was to put your jewels at risk
and now she's wrapped herself around him
how can a woman twist about like that
something in what she's doing
seems to make me sweat

look what about those other two
mincing up and down and eye to eye
this isn't just a tango it is watching at a flame
licking every burning touch
made by a restless pair of roaming hands
and can you see the way
she seems to climb him
from the ground up

up

up

up

until he's holding her
nose to nose she's right there in his face

Frank Prem

I can't dance the tango
I am strictly still a watching man
and if I'm ever going to tango
I think I better make a booking
for some lessons

October 2001

A Random Alphabetical

the loneliness of ironing boards

there is another new ironing board
in the back of my car
it has been there for two days
I don't want to move it

each time I depart
I ensure the essentials

clothes
washing machine
microwave
kettle and iron
electric frying pan
a little cutlery
a little crockery
bed and linen
table and chairs and settee
vacuum cleaner
books in boxes
files and computer

each time I overlook the ironing board

I buy a new one and know

when I stand it up inside the house
against a wall with an available power-point
I will be alone

October 2002

the new love

but I'm in love ma
isn't that great
I haven't been in love
in a long time

well I don't know
I haven't thought about it
I suppose it could get messy
everyone carries baggage
I've got baggage too
we'll work that out

what do you mean
how much in love am I
I'm totally in love
full on
I can't compare this love
with the last one
or the one before
it doesn't work like that
I'm sorry but no
it doesn't

what are you saying ma
we're just starting
she's wonderful
I don't want to think about what happens
when something goes wrong
I want to think that nothing will go wrong
I want to bask in that feeling
so let's not discuss
when it all goes wrong

yes I know
I've got a bad track record
can we change the subject
religion doesn't come into it
I'm not religious and she can be
whatever she wants to be

A Random Alphabetical

ah crikey
don't jump straight to christenings
it's not going to happen all right
no it's not

look she's just a girl I've been seeing
we like each other
ok
it's really nothing more than that

no
I don't suppose it's all that serious
anyway
I don't think you'll be meeting her ma

well I was going to bring her around
to say hello
but
we probably won't be seeing each other
much longer

the reviewer

why relief
he asked himself

it wasn't *better*
sometimes worse
always
always
less

so why the feeling of relief

like a third person -
a reviewer -
hovering above
he looked back and down
at himself

how good it had been

how hard he found it to speak
what was in his head
to say it aloud
as though the sound of the words
would turn everything into overblown reality
or prove the falsehood

every good thing magnified
to impossible goodness

every negative grown large
to loom insurmountable

how the unspoken could be ignored
changed if need be
or hugged in a warmth
that had never been aspired to
could never be uttered aloud
for fear

he looked at her
how she needed
to hear him

his thoughts

his feelings

his reassurance

how he had tried sometimes
to give her what she had needed

the way it made him sweat
shake in discomfort
like a confrontation
with the unformed part of himself

so much angst
for what was
really
so very little
but
beyond what he could find

he looked again
at the incomplete
mental tally

the good things

the deficiencies

his capacity to change

the likelihood now
of ever needing to

this relief is an unsatisfying form but
review
remains an internal process
ongoing

February 2003

the startle reaction

now my first instinct is to keep my eyes away
middle distance is the safest gaze
sort of talk around her
keep a little barrier-bubble in place

but at the same time I'm wondering
why do that
what does it matter if I loosen up a bit
check out the eyes and the bod
offer a sparkle of my own
pull the belly in
adopt a wise tone
watch what happens

see there's years of conditioning
behind an encounter like that
all those years of being spoken for
and a non-contestant
come into the play
rules of engagement have been forgotten
aeons ago
it's a scary situation

she seems nice enough
anxious to make contact
fresh arrival on the scene
it feels good to laugh with someone new
to make little decisions:

> *how much information to share*
> *what re-invention of myself to enact*
> *to stay awhile and drink it all up*

it's not so bad really
an unburdening

A Random Alphabetical

but that first reaction
is to shiver and shake
like a startled rabbit caught in the headlights

my word yes
sooner or later
I need to do some work on that

October 2002

the world's greatest lover

she said

> *I think you must be*
> *the world's best lover*
> *he could hear voice rising*
> *in vibration through his chest*
> *to get inside his head*

she said

> *you care more for me than for yourself*

he said nothing
but considered what it is
that constitutes truth
kissed the top of her head
stretched his arms further around her

~

she said

you must be
the worlds best lover
you don't change
always give me what I want

she said

> *I think you're afraid to ask*
> *for yourself*

he wondered about that
if she was right
knowing she might be
hugged himself tight inside
said nothing

~

she said

> *you might be*
> *the worlds best lover*
> *but you never give*
> *anything of yourself*
> *I never know what's going on*
> *inside your head*

she said

> *it's good it's great*
> *just sometimes I want be*
> *in there with you*
> *do you know what I mean*

he looked at her

frowned

opened his mouth
to tell her a story
of himself
closed it again
feeling the shortness of his breath
and his heartbeat

~

she said

> *you were a great lover*
> *the best*

kissed him on his cheek
waited

he held her close in a hug
tight for a moment
gazed out to the bay
and the water
behind her shoulder
not thinking anything
turned to leave

noticed his breath
came easier today

February 2003

thinking about hands

I think about hands a lot
mine are soft and have a great capacity
for delicacy I'm told
in some ways it may be true
that I see aspects of the world through touch
through fingertips with eyes closed
so much can be revealed
a tasting of textures and response to pressure
rough and smooth   hot and cold
wet and dry   soft and hard
making intimacy a living thing that is physically real
while shaping mental images and sensations
that become response triggers and pathways
to satisfaction and realisation

I think about hands a lot
with horror at the creeping disturbance of skin
by recurrence of watery pustules rising like bubbling mud
over two days to burst
and form dead slough patches
painful and bleeding cracked ugliness
unfit either to touch or be touched
a kind of pre-leprosy
unclean   *unclean*
spreading from digit to digit
causing shy unwillingness to explore or to feel
the texture-less shame
of a sickness of the extremities
hidden only by skillful furtiveness

I have been thinking
about the little finger of my right hand
there are small watery pustules rising
some skin has been shed and a painful crack
has opened up along the line of the first joint

in my kitchen I have a sharpened knife

I have been thinking about that a lot lately

August 2001

to skoll the milk

She said,

> I won a skolling contest once,
> when I was travelling overseas.
> People placed bets on it.
> I forget what I won,
> but the last thing they expected
> was for a young woman,
> hardly more than a girl really,
> to out-skoll the blokes.
>
> It's a skill I learned when I was small.
> I used to sneak to the fridge at night
> to drink milk, straight out of the bottle.
> Did you do that too, when you were small?
> Well,
> you know how, if you suck the bottle too hard,
> you get a mouthful and have to gulp,
> while the suction catches your lips
> then makes a pop, or a hiss,
> when you break the seal?
> My mother would hear me
> and come out to lecture me, every time.
>
> So I practiced
> and learned.
>
> You have to open your oesophagus to
> let the milk slide down,
> without forcing the reflex
> that makes your throat constrict
> in a swallow,
> and without making a sound. Learn to breathe
> while you're doing it.
> Don't let the suction build.

Frank Prem

*I keep my throat open. I draw air
through my nose.*

*That's the way
to get the milk down.*

November 2002

urgency x 2

I didn't study urgency in high school

meet Brian
he's a guy
a friend or something like that
he robbed a bank you know

took the money from his family and the town
and blew it all before they caught him up
and asked him politely
to leave now

he's still around
but doesn't advertise the days
he'll be staying
at his father's place
but sometimes Bill will tell me quietly
that Brian's back in town
and I tell him to say hi from me
we never meet in person
he's much too fast

I didn't study urgency in high school

meet Louisa
she's a girl
I used to think sweet thoughts about
but she never saw me

took her chances with a boy who drove
too loud around the streets and she didn't last
her desk was emptied out
and she was gone

I heard she turned out bitter
from a nephew who didn't know about the past
he thought her a simple tyrant
but I can still recall
the day she turned sixteen
with dark hair bobbed and her eyes aglow
from a kiss across the old school fence
I don't think we'll meet
she was always way too fast

and I never studied urgency

January 2001

wake up

Waking up too tired
Waking without a kiss
Wake without a hug or hold
Waking up to this!

I'm waking to my troubles
Waking up again
Waking to another day
Waking without end.

I'm waking and I'm weary
I'm waking to the cold
I'm waking and I'm lonely
This waking up gets old.

Wake up! Where is passion?
Wake up! Where is fire?
Wake up – where's my lover?
Wake up - no desire.

Wake up again tomorrow
Wake up, much like today
Wake up in the nighttime
Wake up - no more to say.

July 1998

Frank Prem

yellow walls and greying curtains

in my little house the colours
are various shades of faded away

yellow streaks from years of
nicotine laid down
in half-length runs and smears
by an old lady
with a habit

of living inside an easy chair
for so long she hardly knew
the passing of the weeks
or that seasons go by in moments
while her son looked in on odd days
as good lads should
to see her
until the time came

in my little house the curtains
hang in an attitude of mourning

small flowers under dust gone
grey from a
long while of watching
an old lady
out of a habit

draped around a greasy glass
letting light enter like a cry
from all the passing weeks and years
of seasons
and the sun she saw
on some odd days
was spring again
until the time came

A Random Alphabetical

and in my little house
a scrubbing brush and water
will clean the walls
and make the windows shine
curtains with grey flowers
will be thrown away today
for a brighter light and another season
of springtime
little children
and laughter in connecting hallways
until the time comes
for me to live inside an easy chair
under fading colours and mournful curtains
and then at last
to go

February 2001

Whimsy

Whimsy

a new calendar

on the first of opportunity
seize the day

on the second of chances
confront risk

on the third of cautions
peer around each corner

on the fourth of actions
pursue the great

on the fifth of inadequacy
rue what you cannot

on the sixth of decisions
you may be sure

on the seventh of appearances
sackcloth is unbecoming

on the eighth of deceptions
who will really know

on the ninth of assertions
speak as you believe

on the tenth of signs
comb through omens

on the eleventh of questions
choose your meanings

on the twelfth of outcomes
it will be done

February 2003

a primer on image

he said

> you need to smile more
> you often look more stern
> and worried
> than I know you to be
> you come across to others
> as formidable
> it intimidates people who need to trust you

she said

> do you think I look worried
> it's just that he said that I do
> and that it scares people
> I think he was giving me a little primer
> on the subject 'image is everything'

I said

> smile

and repeated it
at every unguarded moment
for an hour
until she laughed

April 2003

before winter

while the days are yet a flourish
in the mornings with the lazy ray of sun
that rides above the current cold
of winter breath
there is a puff of cloud
no more
until
a blinking of the eyes has passed
and grey is come from nowhere
over-filling blue and the immediate surrounds

I will dance upon the green
of luffing grasses
stooped in the act of making wind-puffed
ripple waves
almost sleeping
for the days are growing short
and cool
too cool above the ground

but watch me rise
a leap
to make the sound of clicking heels
and the devil
may he care
for I do not
I am preoccupied
among the drumming rhythms of my feet
to patterns I imagine
with the vigour of a flourish
oh these lazy zephyrous days

come hold my hand and dance you
with me now
before the heavy breath
of winter
sets a weight upon our shoulders
and the season bears us down

June 2002

limericks

A flea and a fly, enroute to Peru,
were distracted, while flying, by an old,
lamby stew.
They landed to eat it,
but were almost defeated
by the waving, green mould that it grew.

Eeeeeewwwwwweeeeee!!!!

~

Aunt Molly, from South Yackandandah,
had a beard that she called Alexander.
If she twirled it around
her three fingers, she found
she could swing from the bull-nosed verandah.

~

My father leads a most musical troup
of ost-e-rich singers who wear
motorbike boots.
Between adjustment of leathers,
and shaking their feathers,
the squawking is not worth two hoots.

January 2001

minty man

Minty man, Minty man
Eat all the Minty's that you can
When you have
Your friends to tea
Give them Minty's all for free!
Minty man, Minty man
Eat all the Minty's
That you can.

Chocolate cake, chocolate cake,
I love the chocolate that you bake.
When I go
To cut a slice
A big fat one is mighty nice!
Chocolate cake, chocolate cake,
I love the chocolate
That you bake.

July 1998

ode to a chip

Let's sing a sad song
for the loss of a chip.
It fell from three fingers
that had a bad grip.

It landed in water
splashed from the pool,
so I stood up and squashed it.
Well, what else could I do?

October 2000

sentimental love you

I'm being silly! Just a sentimental . . .
(Love you)
You probably think that I'm that kind of guy.
But until I opened up my eyes and saw you.
I hardly knew that life was passing by.

You'll tell me now that I should go and . . .
(Love you)
But I could never leave your side, I'm here
to stay.
I'll stick as close as chewing gum,
or blue tac, or tape,
I couldn't live a day with you away.

When they see you on the streets,
the guys all . . .
(Love you)
They don't believe you're going out with me.
They stare as we go by in sheer amazement.
They can see we're just as happy as can be.

It's come as quite a shock that you could . . .
(Love me)
It's the last thing I expected you to do.
But now I've seen the light of love
that lights up in your eyes,
And it's just as well, cause, I Love You!

July 1998

someone still awake?

Is there a little one
In the house, tonight?
Is there a little one
Not sleeping?

Is there a little one
Needs holding tight?
Is there a little one
Needs safekeeping?

I'll take you in my arms this night
I'll hold you, close to me
I'm holding you till morning light
Safe here, wait and see

And I'll rock you a little
Hold you close
Just till you settle
And your eyes are closed

I'll keep you here
Till we see the sun
I'll hold you, darlin
Little one.

Is there someone here
That's still awake?
Is there someone here
Eyes open?

Is there someone here
Needs to feel me close?
Is there someone here
Dreams broken?

I'll keep you near, till sleep creeps in
Stay warm, and close to me
I'll hold you here, against my skin
Hold, my darlin, to me

And I'll hold forever
Till the end of time
Close your eyes
Everything's just fine

I'll stay with you
Till your sleeping's done
I'll stay my darlin
Little one.

November 1998

Whimsy

what's the good of a birthday

What's the good of a birthday?
(Robin's older by a year)
I'd like to have the first say
To make the situation clear.

It's birthday time – let's celebrate
(Doesn't happen each day in a week)
We'll sing and dance and stay up late
Till morning starts to peek.

Congratulations, birthday boy
We're here to wish you well
Gather up your birthday toys
Let's make this party yell!

And who's the star attraction?
Who is this party for?
Who's the one, whose birthday fun
Just makes us all want more?

We'll sing a song for a special day
A day that's bright with sun
We don't want rain for your birthday
We'll let nothing spoil the fun!!

July 1998

when's daddy coming home?

when's daddy coming home?
When's daddy coming home?
He's been away for two whole nights
And I'm feeling all alone.

I miss my daddy so
Why did he have to go?
Why'd he have to up and leave me
Sitting here and feeling needy?

You wouldn't *THINK* he'd be so long
You wouldn't think he'd be so long
He's been away for *TWO WHOLE NIGHTS*
Do you think that something's wrong?

I wish that he'd come back
That I could see him down the track
I wish my dad would come and see
Oh, just how much he means to me!

When's daddy coming home?

July 1998

writing in the moon

shall I write for you
dear reader
the way a fish might do
in swirls and circles
through the water
barely faint disturbance
to the placid surface

all energy
under-current

alternative
the wagtail
curlicues and exclamations
spattered all across the page

aura-format memoranda
of an excitement
hard contained

should I pen
my name in sparkler red
and orange
a continuous flow
of letters
until the glow fades
and you cannot see me
writ before you
anymore

ought I for you
as the feather
quilling in
a free-float of words

that gentle
around suggested meanings
and take their time
to reach a point

but pretty
so very pretty
on their wafted way

perhaps you'd care
to puff them back
a never concluded
sentence suspended
as a mystery in air

or better
if I etch in echoes
of the words you say
you say you say
paraphrase
to let you read on paper
that I can hear you
clean and clear
and clear
but ever
more
faintly

perhaps a smelt
the way the sun
imprints
through heat and sear
burnt like rage
at the height of noon

but no

the lunar sphere has words
that seem to me
more elegant

silver
was always more
the colour
I wrote best

Whimsy

I will in silver

the way the moon

January 2003

Beach and Water

Beach and Water

a stretch of the sand

Appeared in PK List Featured Poets, December 2000

stretching out
golden in the light
away to the edge of vision

contours and ripples
where the waters have come and gone
to shape a resting place
at low tide

before the waves begin
washing higher with every beat
roaring loud
as the wind cries out

then moving again
in the rhythm and play
of a restless building up
until taken like a breath withheld
for a trembling moment
before the ebb begins

and there she lies for me
reaching out in ripple lines
to the edge of light
as a line of gold
and contours at low tide

July 2000

Frank Prem

a sunset on port phillip

Published in The Lakes and Longbeach Gazette, May 2000 edition.

I think the sun
is bleeding
as it falls
beyond the edge
of rippled water
at the end
of day

the voices of children
squealing laughter
from the sand
give no hint
of recognition
that the sun
is made of blood
and falling
somewhere beyond the bay

March 2000

adventure moon

when the moon is high
we could sail from Aspendale
over the waters of the bay

let's aim for Sorrento
or Point Nepean

the stars will shine above
and in reflection
from the restless waves

wind and salt on your face
the taste and feel of adventure
for you and me

take the tiller
while I stand in the bows
aim left of the channel lights
and sail away let's

sail away tonight
when the moon is high

2002

at the jetty

at the jetty
in the waters washing round the piles,
a fish or two

there was a time
just a year or two (or was it ten?)
back when the waters around these pylons
were dead
it's reassuring to be able to look down now
and see a couple of tiddlers swimming
and to watch the little kids
getting excited to see them
or trying hard to catch them with
fishing lines rigged up
by their dads
they get very intense sometimes
like it's the most important thing in the world
to land one of those small fish

the break-water waves
washing over rocks
with nothing else to do

I read somewhere that it is all man-made
and I guess that's true
it must have been quite a feat to lay out
all those rocks to control the water flow
and make sure of sheltered inlets
the bay responded of course
and it's fascinating to watch
when there's an injection of money
from somewhere
and they dredge up sand
from a kilometer off-shore
and pump it onto what's left of the beach

Beach and Water

I think they call it re-nourishment
but I believe it is due
to the bay
taking revenge

tight wires
sing along the masts of yachts, tied up
and rocking too

the yacht club looks quite pretty
with all its boats
anchored in the morning light
they come in all sorts of colours but
as a group
I always have an impression
of gleaming whiteness
I never think of them as being sea-craft
because they seem to belong
just where they are
at anchor in the marina
in a collective of white
bobbing gently
with the motion of calmed waves

a salty breeze
ruffling feathers on the squatting gulls
asleep right through
they seem so refined
until they open their mouths and screech
or fix one of those beady eyes
on you in a hungry stare

it is better to watch their smooth shapes
and the way they can sleep
while standing on one leg
and to marvel at the numbers
that gather together

just occasionally
a better spectacle presents itself
when two or three gannets come by
and present a spectacle through their diving
for fish a short way offshore
so fast and so deep
but the gulls will do if there's no better show
on offer

and the sun
is shining brightly
on the quiet of the watching pair
of me and you

thanks for coming with me tody
it's nicer in company

August 2000

Beach and Water

bay watch

on arrival
it is already dark but the expanse of water
is visible from this balcony
the bay is quiet but a soft lapping of waves
has a disproportionate and demanding
loudness

small wavelets show a phosphorescent flash
of white and blue brightness
then disappear

later . . .

the waves in front of me are dark
wearing shades of stealth and invisibility
but to my right the city lights
form rippled streaks
scribble-lines
reaching towards my overseeing perch
and giving life to the surface of the water

on the left the reflections
are a muted orange dullness
with no suggestion of force or power

I wonder at these changes
and look out
across the restlessness of the bay

July 2001

Frank Prem

black rock by bicycle

I would ride a bicycle to Black Rock
in the morning to see if you
were dancing on the waters
in the softer sun,
when it is fine and cool,
before the heat begins the day.
I would ride.

As the bay moves it is
shining in a million ways,
with every shaping wave that rises
up, only to fall again
after a momentary gleaming,
and I believe I will see you there,
dancing on the waters
like a child that splashes
puddles on the way
to school, twirling around
with your arms wide
open, calling me to you.
A peddle turn
and I will be there
to feel the flowing of
your robe run over me,
and taste the spray
from each rising footstep.

I would ride my bicycle to Black Rock
if I could see you there
in the early, softened morning light,
when it is fine and cool.
I would ride for you.

January 2001

cleansing salted water

tasting hard water
in the bay
slow rolling
and gentle rocking
to stray glimpses
of a moon
that's hide and seeking
through the black
of stormy clouds

falling showers
of light tattoo rain
reach down
to the warm
of a lowly tide

in early morning
I'm half seeing
where I think you are

sliding in and
out of sight
as the shadows move
the sound
of washing waves
is an illusion
of distance

until the soft contrast
of exploration
above and below
the water-line
seeks out
a source of taste
for lips and tongue
to cleanse away
salted water

March 2000

Frank Prem

cresting waves and white foam

when you were young did you
ride on cresting waves
taking journeys atop the breakers?
power and majesty
flowing underneath your feet
did you stand up or did you bow
before the foam that swallows the weakness
of those who've fallen away
in the path of something higher
than they ever dreamed to fly or ride
with only a tiny link
to keep them hovering so proximal to peril?

I am standing to my hips in cold
feeling the tug of something old and strong
dragging me to submerge
my thoughts in a swirl of tumbled chaos
but I don't need to feel that way
I can stand and watch and I can walk away
any moment that I want release
I don't think I will climb the mountain waves
I'll stay a paddler in the shallows
never getting too deep
and never plunging over my head

incoming waves ride on top of the ebb
with fingers of foam surfing to the shore
I've watched them for hours
to see the way it's done
but I have no insight into staying afloat
without a board or a raft or a lifeguard
holding on
my place is in the shallows
watching daredevil riders
on cresting waves and white foam

October 2000

digging furrows

I am digging furrows in the bay
with my hand opened wide
to form the blue-green jets of dragging water
raising spray white and high
as I spin
on sand that accepts my twisting feet
and offers self as anchor

I am making music
with air that follows a plunging hand
below waterline
backwards and forwards
until the bubbles have expired
and the movement is complete

bathers think me a strange one
turning around and around
engrossed in the patterning of air
dragged beneath the water
more like to child than man

but they have only come to swim
and to frolic
while I
am making furrows and music

February 2001

Frank Prem

in blue

Published in Manifold Magazine #39 (UK) September 2001

with the dying sun before me
and water barely to my knees
I am among a gaggling clutter
of clinging children dragging at me
while I stand solid to watch
the yellow-white of cloud lines
streaking from the deeper oranges
and reds of the westernmost sky
with its ball of vibrant vermillion
and the silhouette of promontory trees
stark black but glowing
from the fire lit behind them

with the liquid sun at my back
I am turned to the east where
the cavorting bodies of bathers
between me and dry land are shaded
with the rich and changing hues
of a descending day and in vivid blue
on the shore sits a youth with cropped hair
and small sideburns that I can see
clearly despite the coloured light
I have to look hard and closely
before I can tell
it is not a crimson boy in blue
that it is you
sitting on the sand and watching me

as I write and remember
there is a red burn still spotting my eyes
from the fading sun off the beach at Mentone
sand grits between my toes and
I can taste salt when I lick at my lips and hold
the remains of an image of molten colours
but you are at home and vivid in blue

February 2001

millennial morning

there is light on the water of the bay
even in the depths of darkness
small breaking waves show white
and the sound of their rolling to the beach
is a calming constancy
the sound of forever

there are different shades of dark
in these vast waters
perhaps reflections of city lights
perhaps the sky itself

the beach is deserted except for we two
who stand to watch and to wait
in the strange stillness after a night
so full of sound and noise
colour and light
cheery anticipation

behind my shoulder the sky
changing almost imperceptibly
but it is definite
the question is finally answered
at least for us
here on the beach
on the bay
at the end of the night

even on this of all days
dawn comes

January 2000

no poetry on the bay

no poetry lives on the bay today
there are only images to report
before they disappear
across the sky

like the plastic bag

last seen
it was one hundred feet high and sailing
towards Edithvale
lifted on the folly of a fickle wind
that trailed lightly across green water
rippling in easy rhythms
of movement

adrift
above a hundred small whiting
still in school

clouds stray across the blue
thinning to a subtle suggestion
beneath a sun
that retains warmth to spite autumn
even as the water pays respect
to the time of year
in currents of coldness
bearable but threatening
chill in only a week
or two

bag and breeze
overfly squealing gulls
that wheel and turn then hover
in seeming leisure
before decent
to the feast of a dozen
scattered loaves
that a discerning eye can tell
are no more than a day old

Beach and Water

and assuredly free
to any takers

no poetry on the bay
but images disappearing

March 2001

reclaiming mentone

there is earth moving equipment
on the beach

out of character
on the packed golden granules
leaving the deep furrows
of yellow tray-truck
and matching front-end loader
(with scoop)

the noise is pure diesel -
grumbling power -
to take accumulated sand
from the distant groyne
where it stockpiles each year
and deliver it
to the place where we stand
adding an annual nourishment
and contouring

a wind has risen
to further spoil the evening

there is a cold air
that does not suit
the sunshine
washing over us

a brightly coloured chill but
the time is coming
perhaps only days away
when it will be warm . . .

it will be hot

then we too will perform
an annual nourishment

Beach and Water

we will reclaim
the waters
on the sand at Mentone
this will -
once again -
be ours

2001

sabres at patterson river

a flotilla of flat-bottomed sabres
red triangled teeth atop the white
of a single sail
forty strong and tacking as a shoal -
tightly bunched -
with a solitary straggler to the rear
and one that is running hard to port
and pointed
at the piece of flour-soft yellow sand
marked out as my personal territory
by a towel and a book
and the clear blue overlay of cloudless sky

~

I have waited these three
slow-passing months
of damp and lukewarm pseudo-summer
for such a day of unambiguous stinging heat
and the salt water is already autumn sharp
in a rapid-cooling contrast
to the dry temperature
concentrated inches above the asphalt
of a baking carpark
and the bleached loose grains
that lie above water level

the slap of small-wave motion –
enough to force the awkwardness
of balance on tip-toes

with each rise in depth towards the nethers –
is worth endurance for the clean freshness
of first submersion and aquatic acclimatisation

~

Beach and Water

the wind is on the rise
the water shows a small white-headed chop
and is less attractive for the uncommitted
sabre teeth are sentinel poles
and singing metal lines
pulled up before the club-rooms and above
the high-water mark
various parties are packing up
and going home
despite the forty five degrees of sun
that still remains before curtain fall

on this Patterson River
of powdered beach

of gulls
and boats
navigating the river-mouth channel
in search of a safe berth

a broken trail of bright and silver
shivers in their wake
reflects the last remnants
of a Sunday on the bay

March 2002

Frank Prem

saltless autumn

Appeared in Map of Austin poetry E-zine #183-1 May 2001

I miss the sands of summer
that yield to the probing of feet
digging into an anchorage
against the movement of blue water
clear enough to see the golden embrace

salt tasting my lips

I stood in the wash of rising tides
felt the cool lick at my skin

and upon my face the release
of a shallow dive to freedom
under rocking waves of comfort

salt wash upon my lips

I am rue in this biting cold
that tells me there is now
a numb pain in that water
gleaming chilled green
and withholding invitation

saltless lips in autumn

April 2001

shallows

the wavelets are breaking
with a following wind
over the shallow field of rocks
that serves for a beach at Williamstown
they break at speed   . . .

leaping white
into the air
like a school of small fish
surrounded by predators
fleeing terrified
between elements

elsewhere
a rippling of the water implies
the presence of a large fish-
perhaps a skate or ray

there is an impression
of shallows life
but this too is illusion
merely a flat rock disturbing tide flow

so typical of the pretentious willy-town
place of shallows
and lies

December 2001

Frank Prem

straight road to brighton

she will never drive directly to Brighton
even though the road from here
is close and fast

she would think it wasted time
however short the trip
when there is a beach road
overlooking the restlessness of water
and white-faced waves
breaking in a long curved row
between the sand of Mentone
and the red cliffs of the bluff
at Sandringham

white yellow-streaked birds
plunge down into the waters of the Bay

these are solitary
lonely divers
who follow the arc blue
of a rising wave
she can see these birds
from a roadside carpark
beside the beach road to Brighton
and will watch for minutes at a time
as they disappear below the water

I rarely drive by the highway now
there are sea birds here
and breaking waves
I have learned at last
that this is the straightest road
to travel

November 2001

sunset goodnight

down, I'm walking
to the place where
water meets the sand
and the game is only
spreading wavelets
across my footprints
with the tide

one moment I'm there
and at the next look
I may never have been

there is another dying
in the distance
it is leaving
with a shimmer
that I
have to watch
to the last red glow
in the sails of a late yacht
that's making it's way
back home

sometimes it's like that

a little bit late-side
but finding a way to home

I shouldn't have come here
there are places that I need to be
but
you know the way it is
you know the hold
of this place
with it's lapping of waves
the sand on my feet
and the sunset
goodnight

this place is a hold
when the sun sets goodnight

2001

the weight of water

and the empty moments
are like the weight of water

I lie suspended
as I fall down

gentle
but
down

it is so far

April 2004

this is mine

Featured in the e-zine Caught in the Net 3 May 2001

I am making this my own,
from gun metal blue salt water
to orange fruiting of the sun.

I am ankle deep in the sands of low tide,
running out fast
in the chop of a wind
that has raised the heads white,
up on driving waves
full of fizz in the black
of a night rising,
with the moon
shining in a line going out forever
to the last of daylight.

This is all mine

March 2001

waiting for the paint to dry

I am waiting for the paint to dry. Watching
the gulls batten down against
a breeze that isn't cold yet,
but shows promise.

The wash of three sandbanks
is captured in the picture
and the sky of blue and cloudy
haze above the waters
stretches to a long time around
the corner of the Black Rock
promontory.

There is no yellow for the
emergence of the foreshore.
The tube must be in the basket
still on the kitchen bench.
We can bring it another time,
but the sand might speak more of brown,
and we'd better bring the basket
to be sure.

The paint is dry and the gulls
are huddling closer,
seeming to feel a collective need
to preen
before the strength of a rising wind.
Time to go.
There is nothing more beyond
colour in a basket.
Let's go home.

March 2001

westgate, the city, the bay

there are other
newer bridges
but it is Westgate
that is Melbourne

this night
the red lights are flashing
to slow traffic
between raised central spires
that climb into the sky
almost vanishing
a periodic pinpoint
and ward for stray flyers

at the apex
I can see to Frankston
perhaps beyond
it is eighty kilometres around
but it is mine to claim
with a glance

so many lights
this city is a universe
of star twinkles at ground level
doubled by reflection
and I am above them all

blues and yellows and reds
neon signs larger
taller brightnesses
intruded upon symmetry
until the gaze slips by St Kilda

around the curve
almost flying above terra
or short-cut skipping
across the stilled waters
of the bay

Beach and Water

to alight momentarily
at Black Rock
Mentone
Aspendale
Chelsea
Carrum
Frankston

Portsea a fade beyond

drive slowly
from here you might see
the pulse of my city

May 2002

After Words

Index of Poems

A

a bad week 203
a circlet of pearls 206
acknowledging original sources 26
a cloud beneath the cross 5
a contact for astro-man 207
a day in the life - october 4 - NPD 120
ad libbing 27
adventure moon 291
afraid of weather 28
after 'till the next time' 29
a full confession 6
a funny thing, memory 7
a kind of love poem 11
alive 30
almost sufficient 33
a lot 'o week 13
an absentee; a companion 210
a new calendar 271
a nightshirt (for when it gets cold) 14
a poet at war 15
a primer on image 272
a reading 16
a shoe of frustration 17
a shooting star in emergency 19
a sound like moth wings beating 23
asthmatic refrain 31
a story for my lawyer 25
a stretch of the sand 289
a sunset on port phillip 290
ATT #2 - almost sufficient 33
ATT #14 those hours 34
ATT #20 - a heel on lino 35
ATT #26 the plot lost too 36
ATT #33 - between this and the next 38
ATT #51 - growth by infusion 39
at the jetty 292
attraction (by the bottle) 212

a wicked man (just trust me) 209

B

baghdad rain, or a movie? 40
bath-time for boys 41
bay watch 295
beautiful pictures (1) 42
beautiful pictures (2) 43
before winter 273
believe the stars 45
between this and the next 38
black rock by bicycle 296
blood and feathers 46
by silence 48

C

calling late 213
change of seasons 51
choosing between guitars 54
cleansing salted water 297
cloudy face prayer 214
clues 56
colostomy song 57
coloured sand dancing 58
comfort movies 215
concert 59
confusing realities (a sound of thunder) 60
craving 62
cresting waves and white foam 298
currency 63

D

damp spirits 216
digging furrows 299
doing a shirt (steam) 64
drowning slapnoea 65

E

enclosed by cloud 219
expression of interest sought (apply within) 218

eyes awake 67

F

faeces rag 68
family law 69
filling the quota 70
first week in the month 71
flying 72
flying home 220
fragment 73
from afar 74
fuck you fever poem 221

G

getting a grip 75
getting close to venice 76
goodnight 77
got no rhythm 79
growth by infusion 39

H

habits die hard 83
hammered gold and gilded tin 84
homemaking in adverse conditions 181

I

I am the place 223
identifying the golubs 183
if a rialto crumble 86
if the sky should fall 87
I know 85
illumination - my turn 89
I might move closer 224
in absentia 90
in blue 300
interior decoration 182
interior designs 91
it's valentine's 93

J

just friends 95

K

kiss me 225

L

letters and words 97
lighthorse man in my collection 98
like almonds 226
like a stereo out of hell 99
limericks 275
liqour kiss 100
liquor song 228
little boy blue 229
long distance love affair 101

M

master of nothing new 105
maybe elvis 230
middle winter blues 107
millennial morning 301
minty man 276
mis-arrangement of flowers 231
miss it a bit 109
mizzle down 111
morning metaphor 112
moving air 113
mystery and tedium 232

N

nearly love 234
nervousness 114
no poetry on the bay 302
no telling 235
not really fragile 117

O

observing beautification (through force of habit) 119

ode to a chip 277
on introduction 123
over lunch 237

P

paper aeroplanes 124
perfume? 125
pigeon-trification 179
plastic spirits 126
plat-ing 127
politics personal 128
pot pourri 129
predator 130
premature flight 185
pretensions 132
prickling eyes 133

R

reclaiming mentone 304

S

sabres at patterson river 306
saltless autumn 308
scotch sleeping 238
search for my soul 137
sentimental love you 278
shallows 309
shoes 139
short-term tenancy 140
single drek 141
single male shopper 143
sleep in his head 146
snapping pictures 148
solace 244
some dancing 246
someone still awake? 279
staying 149
still three o'clock (franky's not at home) 151
storm bringer 152
stormy weather 153
straight road to brighton 310

sunset goodnight 311
sweat dribble down 154

T

tango 247
ten signs of life 240
the fluent pen 155
the kiss 156
the loneliness of ironing boards 249
the messenger 157
the negative weight of craters on the face of the moon 159
the new love 250
the new west: a ride on the st albans line 195
the new west: a touch of succulence on barkly street 189
the new west: community health in the new west 196
the new west: main street west 191
the new west: new west 198
the new west: reverse parking at three thirty 193
the old familiar 161
the reviewer 163, 252
the ride 166
the spread 167
the startle reaction 254
the weight of water 313
the world's greatest lover 256
thinking about hands 259
this is mine 314
time to dance 169
to make it worthwhile 171
tonight blues 173
to skoll the milk 261

U

unceasing vigilance 184
unfamiliar affections 147
urgency x 2 263

W

waiting for the paint to dry 315
wake up 265
watchful credit 174

wedding song 175
westgate, the city, the bay 316
what's the good of a birthday 281
when's daddy coming home? 282
whispered voice (over and over) 176
writing in the moon 283

Y

yellow walls and greying curtains 266

Author Information

Frank Prem has been a storytelling poet since his teenage years. He has been a psychiatric nurse through all of his professional career, which now exceeds forty years.

He has been published in magazines, online zines, and anthologies in Australia, and in a number of other countries, and has both performed and recorded his work as spoken word.

He lives with his wife in the beautiful township of Beechworth in North East Victoria, Australia.

Connect with Frank

Find Frank at his website www.FrankPrem.com, or through Social Media online at Facebook, X (Twitter), Instagram and YouTube.

Other Published Works

Free Verse Poetry

Small Town Kid (2018)
Devil In The Wind (2019)
The New Asylum (2019)
Herja, Devastation - With Cage Dunn (2019)
Walk Away Silver Heart (2020)
A Kiss for the Worthy (2020)
Rescue and Redemption (2020)
Pebbles to Poems (2020)
The Garden Black (2022)
A Specialist at The Recycled Heart (2022)
Ida: Searching for The Jazz Baby (2023)
From Volyn to Kherson (2023)
Alive Is What You Feel (2023)
White Whale (2024)
Pilgrim Volume 1 - Illustrated by Leanne Murphy (2024)
A Poetry Archive Volume 1 (2024)
A Poetry Archive Volume 2 (2024)
A Poetry Archive Volume 3 (2024)
A Poetry Archive Volume 4 (2024)

Picture Poetry/Spoken Image

Voices (In The Trash) (2020)
The Beechworth Bakery Bears (2021)
Sheep On The Somme (2021)
Waiting For Frank-Bear (2021)
A Lake Sambell Walk (2021)
A Few Places Near Home (2023)
The Cielonaut (2024)

What Readers Say

Small Town Kid

A modern-day minstrel. Highly recommended.
—A. F. (Australia)

Small Town Kid is a wonderful collection.
—S. T. (Australia)

Devil In The Wind

Trust me, this book will stay with you. Bravo!
—K. K. (USA)

Moving, beautiful, and terrible. I was left with a profound sense of respect, as well as a reminder that we should never take for granted every precious every moment of life.
—J. S. (South Africa)

The New Asylum

Words can't do justice to the emotional journey I travelled in (reading this collection).
—C. D. (Australia)

If I had to pick one book over the past year that has truly resonated with me, this would be it.
—K. B. (USA)

Walk Away Silver Heart

Instantly grips you by the throat in his step-by-step story of survival. Bravo!
—K. K. (USA)

Outstanding!
—B. T. (Australia)

A Kiss For The Worthy

A Celebration of Life Written in Thoughtful Bursts of Poetic Expression
—C. M. C. (United States)

With every verse, I found myself reflecting about myself, my life, and the world.
—K.

Rescue and Redemption

The passion of love in its many forms explored by one for another.
—J. L. (United States)

I've enjoyed every word, every breath. Every moment within the life of these stories.
—C. D. (Australia)

Sheep On The Somme

Museums and archivists take note--sell this in your gift shops, preserve it in your archives. Professors, teachers--share with your students.
—A. R. C. (United States)

(This) book is a beautiful and graphic tribute to all those brave men and women who gave their lives for their countries between 1914 and 1918.
—R. C. (South Africa)

Ida: Searching for The Jazz Baby

I found myself deeply moved by the presentation of Ida's elusive, illusionary life.
—E. G. (United States)

He gives her a depth and vulnerability that the press didn't.
— A. C. (United Kingdom

The Garden Black

Prem creates verse that illuminates our world, its experiences and history.
—S. C. (United Kingdom)

Prem's poetry reminds that life is fragile and fleeting ... both harsh and beautiful.
—D. G. K. (Canada)

A Few Places Near Home

The author has captured many beautiful images in this book, and is a wonderful photographer as well as a poet. This book would make a beautiful coffee table book filled with moving prose to make us ponder with gorgeous accompanying images.
—D. K. (Canada)

www.FrankPrem.com

www.ingramcontent.com/pod-product-compliance
Lightning Source LLC
Chambersburg PA
CBHW052107110526
44591CB00013B/2391